GETTING IT RIGHT
FOR BOYS

Neil Farmer

Featherstone

I would like to dedicate this book t... ...ohn, who was the
very best of what a boy could be – ... top...

Published 2012 by Featherstone Education, Bloomsbury Publishing plc
50 Bedford Square
London
WC1B 3DP

ISBN 978-14081-4071-0

Text © Neil Farmer
Design by Bob Vickers
Cover photographs © Shutterstock
Photographs on pages 27, 66, 70, 77, 83 © Acorn Childcare Ltd, Milton Keynes

A CIP record for this publication is available from the British Library.

Printed in Great Britain by Latimer Trend and Company Ltd

This book is produced using paper that is made from wood grown in
managed, sustainable forests. It is natural, renewable and recyclable.
The logging and manufacturing processes conform to the environmental
regulations of the country of origin.

To see our full range of titles
visit www.acblack.com

Contents

Introduction

In a market flooded with useful books on how to work with young children and ensure they achieve the best they can, is there room for one more?

I like to think that there is – a book not so much to give advice and strategies, but rather to foster discussion and prompt early years practitioners to look deeply at their own views and beliefs on what makes good learning – in this instance for boys. Not everybody will agree with the ideas in this book, but that is the point of it, to promote discussion in schools and settings around meeting the needs of young male learners.

Debate

The key point to debate has to be: *Are our learning environments and our pedagogic beliefs allowing boys to realise their potential?*

Good learning, for all children, occurs when children are a recognised part of the process. This is true of mature learners as well. To learn you have to be cognitively and physically engaged in the process and deep-level learning involves emotional engagement in the job at hand. To learn without context, without opportunity for meaningful application, without a self-realisation of what and why you are doing something is senseless and in no way leads to deep-level internalisation of concepts, skills or knowledge. It also fails to create a disposition to continue learning.

This book will hopefully assist practitioners in analysing their beliefs about learning and to an extent, utilise theory and scientific enquiry to reason why it is that boys are a constant source of worry in terms of their application to learning and their lowering expectations and outcomes.

I shall be looking at brain development and the chemical/hormonal make up of young learners and the impact that these disparate issues have on the ability to learn, the preferred learning style and the age-appropriateness of strategies.

It is important that all those who work with the youngest of children are aware of the multi-faceted issues that have profound effects on developing learning and fostering a positive disposition towards learning. Without this knowledge practitioners and children are stuck in the same cycle, repeating what has not worked and doing more of the same.

From the adult perspective, to self-reflect and analyse one's own performance and entrenched views can, for some, be an unsettling and traumatic experience. It puts under intense scrutiny all that we once held to be true and have consequently reflected in our policy, practice, procedure and routine.

It is my firmly-held belief that it is not the boys who are 'under-achieving' at all. Instead, too many practitioners are underachieving in their policy, provision and practice to meet the diverse needs of all children. They are failing to realise that true inclusive practice entails an appreciation of difference, as it is through this that similarities can be made.

Learning and attainment are measured in ways that mitigate against boys being successful. This is especially true of the Early Years Foundation Stage Profile (2008). In this, summative developmental statements cut across how many young male learners actually learn and more importantly how they *implement* this learning in practical activities that may 'go against the grain' of many practitioners' views on what entails 'good' learning.

Personal background

This book is written from a personal perspective. It contains some theoretical approaches and some research. The crux, however, is to be 'real'. It provides real experiences and tries to put young children's learning in the context where it belongs. This context is sometimes overlooked – children are young once, it is a time of safety and imagination, a time of wonder, excitement, awe and understanding. It should be the best of times, it should be fun.

Professionally I have worked in early years education as a nursery and reception class teacher, advisory teacher, Foundation Stage Consultant and Head of Early Years. This knowledge and understanding, added to previous experiences, has given me great insight into how boys learn and develop into young adults and men. I have undertaken countless visits to settings and schools across the nation; completed School Improvement Partner and Ofsted training; had the pleasure of being a key note speaker at regional and national events and written for national publications.

My passion is with boys' learning and this book is aimed at teachers and practitioners working with children from birth to seven, when the predilection for future learning and self-reflection are crystallising in young brains.

Boyhood memories and school days – a start to the learning process

My junior and secondary education was in an all boys' boarding school, where, through lack of anything purposeful to do (except sport and marching about as part of the Cadet Force), creativity, problem solving and risk taking took centre stage to keep us amused. But more of this later.

I suppose I was extremely fortunate to be born when I was and to go to primary school in the late 1960s and early 1970s. I have very little recollection of the curriculum offered but do have memories of having a very happy time, with lots of 'playing', singing (especially Cat Stevens songs and teachers in long flowing dresses) and finding stuff out. We had copious amounts of freedom, free from adult interference – they were happy times.

On the whole primary education appeared to be about doing, being outdoors and lots of talking. Somewhere along the line I learnt to read, write and add up. I did this quite easily so must have been enjoying the experiences, but mostly I learnt about doing, through experiencing things first-hand and applying that thinking to real-life opportunities.

I remember lots of games that involved team work, counting, scoring, writing and deciphering clues. The joy experienced in constructing the best racing cart – that didn't win, but which we modified and adapted so it would be even better next time. Just think of the cross-curricula links and the utilisation of skills: reading, writing, social interaction, space, shape and measure, problem solving.

There was the sheer pleasure of independence and autonomy, knowing what we were doing and the next step in the process. One would imagine that at this juncture the concepts of 'forwards to basics' (Laevers 2000) and Vygotsky's 'Zone of Proximal Development' (1967) were at the forefront of school thinking. A view on what is possible not the 'what is'. It was a matter of having that freedom to do, so that possibility was the driver behind creativity. A simple change from the 'What is it?' to the 'What could it be?' opens a myriad of intriguing possibilities.

Also back in those salad days we were afforded a mighty amount of freedom, as a group of friends we were out, a long way from home, for an awfully long time. Older children looked after younger children and the youngest watched and listened in awe as the elders climbed trees and built things out of planks of wood and old boxes and told adventure stories and yarns. Learning was about watching, listening, about imitating, innovating and finally inventing.

We had times of intense tedium, when an active, creative mind was needed to relieve the boredom. We needed our imaginations, developed language skills and a sizeable helping of self-reliance. We had to invent our games, our resources were open-ended and reusable despite the context of play. They could become a thousand different things, there to manifestly represent something that we did not have.

It is a sad indictment of modern times that many children are not given these opportunities and consequently lack the imagination of innovation and invention, because the foundations of imitating, watching and listening are not imbedded. As Pie Corbett says 'you cannot create out of nothing' (*Talk for Writing* materials 2008).

Moving to Secondary school, I attended an all boys' boarding school, until the late 1970s when girls were finally admitted and the culture of the school discernibly changed. It was an interesting place. The school was rife with testosterone and dominated by the Sixth Form who were given licence to hand out mandatory punishments to any wayward transgressor, or someone they did not particularly take a liking to. This 'punishment' usually took the form of some physical ordeal or copying tracts from the *Oxford English Dictionary* onto A4 paper, always ensuring there were eight words to a line.

Music was a huge part of my early life, and still is. I could retreat into a safe world of sounds with bands that were lyrically reflecting my emotions. I was a great fan of the Punk movement and the whole philosophy of action – very male orientated, just have a go, put yourself out there and have a go, it might not work, but boy will you find out lots of things along the way. Lyrics by Stiff Little Fingers *'Question everything you're told',* The Jam *'Stop apologising for the things you've never done'* and The Clash *'I'm all lost in the supermarket',* still resonate today and underpin much of my thinking towards learning and teaching.

The school was run on fear and intimidation. If one was remotely weak the hounds would descend, mainly in order to deflect any attention from themselves. I soon learnt who was approachable, affable and friendly and who was not. I learnt this through watching and this is how many boys learn – watching for cause and effect.

Being a boarder I had a fair amount of free time to fill with all sorts of pranks – making up our own entertainment was key: brewing home-brew, making cigarettes out of tea bags, anything to pass the time and add a modicum of excitement to our existence. The school was split between those who did and those who followed. We were, however, all in it together and once the hierarchy had been established, positive relationships were forged. As boys are very physical in nature and the physical changes undergone by youths are quick, this hierarchy was always being challenged. Growth spurts and hormone rushes led to a change in appearance and strength, so roles changed and became more fluid in nature as relationships were cemented.

There are four things that have stayed with me from my school experience:

- How *not* to formally teach children – especially boys.
- How to foster and develop deep and life-long friendships.
- An appreciation of difference, development and acceptance that not all are the same – which we can all learn from each other, there is no hierarchy.
- A sense of self-reliance and confidence.

In an odd way secondary school was very successful for me, not the academic learning and teaching, but the non-curricula ethereal stuff – a sense of morality, fortitude, strength of purpose and character. This, I guess, is the purpose behind schooling and education. It is not about what you achieve, but rather what you have the potential to achieve later in life. It provided me with a sound 'education' but more importantly a series of strategies with which to cope with setback and problems – many of which had been laid down through good early years provision and built upon and revisited as I got older and developed.

The role of the adult

There are many scholarly books and research articles on learning styles and gender difference. They cover brain development, socio-economic and cultural factors, societal expectations and structural change – but many do not deal with the issue at hand – the role of the adult in the whole learning and teaching experience.

Without sensitive, interested and knowledgeable adults (in terms of experience and *know how,* not necessarily theory) the required deep-level children's learning just does not happen. It is a sad fact that too many of our practitioners do not have sufficient practical skill, experience and understanding to back up principle and put it into practice. Learning and teaching is not about delivery, it is about understanding and genuineness, the ability to link concepts and ideas together, to be a true empathetic and critical friend. It is an incredibly complex and difficult role, especially when dealing with the youngest of children where the emotional demands are high. It is even more challenging when dealing with a cohort full of young boys.

What learning opportunities do our settings actually provide for boys? What do we offer boys in terms of stimulation and excitement on a regular basis and for prolonged periods of time? I have known colleagues to become genuinely depressed at the thought of having a boy-heavy cohort – the fear of the unknown, a whole plethora of excitable, active mud-eating monsters! Unfortunately to many it is daunting because the physicality of the learners is juxtaposed with beliefs of what makes *good* learning and the pressure for children to 'achieve'.

While writing this book I have been working with many schools, settings and parents and the common theme that runs through all this work is boys. The ways in which they are different, their physicality, language, emotional needs, attention spans, the environments they require, the space they need for movement and the time they need to become truly involved in learning.

Many of our schools and settings are so routine-heavy they mitigate against the needs of the children, and as a result many children, and more often boys, become disaffected, boisterous and seemingly 'rowdy'. The majority of this behaviour could be curtailed if practitioners were to put the needs of the children first and the routines second.

How boys learn and develop

I have not always been 'in education'. In fact it was something I decided upon after a number of years scouring and searching for my true identity. I genuinely did not have a clue until my mid-twenties as to the direction my life would take. The paths I took led me to careers in construction, shop work, sales – all of which had a common theme – they were journeys, somehow I knew it then although I could not express it. Looking back I suppose I was being a typical boy, with a short concentration span and the need for future challenge – that next step to test myself against. In the words of Laevers (2000) I was searching for the 'flow' when competency equals challenge, where there is the potential to learn and be working at the very edge of one's limits.

I worked mainly with other males. I became fascinated by how they think, what makes them what they are, how they do things and how they respond to each other, I watched and listened to life stories and experiences, laughed with colleagues and became aware of hierarchies and how they operate.

This really was the crystallisation process of all previous experiences actually falling into place and I suddenly became 'aware' of what I should and could be doing. I, like many boys, was not ready for this at

Getting it right for boys

the tender age of 17 or 18. I simply knew that there was something out there that would grab me – so I started to look, to experience and collate life so all my learning started to make some sense to me.

I do feel enormous sympathy for many of our young male learners. The expectation is huge, the requirement to make informed and intelligent decisions is unrealistic for many and the pressure to achieve, conform and put in place systems that are not yet fully developed places enormous stress on young males. Is it any wonder that this particular age group is at most risk of self-harm, depression and at worst suicide?

One of my real pleasures is coaching rugby and watching a group of ego-centric, clumsy, uncoordinated, uncommunicative youngsters develop both physically and cognitively. They gain appreciation of others, forge friendships and in short become 'joined up' and capable of meeting future challenges head on and with a degree of confidence.

What do you believe in?

As a provider for young children's learning it is vitally important to have a clear set of values and a firm vision of what makes good learning in the early years. This needs to be shared with and agreed by all stakeholders as it will underpin everything that you do in terms of provision, expectation, routine and processes. Get this vision wrong and it will have devastating consequences for all young learners, especially those who do not readily fit into, or conform to it, in this instance boys.

Setting out your vision

Circle five or six characteristics you consider most important to encourage in adults and children – this will help to reflect and underpin your belief system.

Also draw a line through those characteristics you would not wish to encourage, or your setting discourages – are there any questions this throws up in line with your vision?

If so what are you going to do about it?

Characteristics you consider important to encourage in adults and children

Adventurous	Energetic
Affectionate	Fearful
Good at guessing	Friendly
Asks questions	Industrious
Athletic	Independent
Careful	Negative
Conforming	Obedient
Competitive	Quiet
Co-operative	Rebellious
Courageous	Refined
Courteous	Receptive
Creative	Risk taking
Critical	Self-confident
Domineering	Self-satisfied
Emotional	Sensitive
Has a sense of humour	Timid
Stubborn	Versatile
Talkative	Well-adjusted

Getting it right for boys

This list is not exhaustive; you may well think of your own adjectives that you wish to bring to the party. Be you a parent, a practitioner or school leader this is a useful exercise in crystallising your vision and values into something far more tangible. It involves all stakeholders in the process and is the catalyst for in-depth discussion and agreed values. The concept is simple: what are the characteristics that you feel important to become a confident life-long learner and consequently what are the characteristics of adults supporting your young learners that you wish to draw upon?

In settings and schools where this has been successful the process has been transparent. Introduce the idea at staff/parents meetings and explain the purpose. Have a large circle on the display board and around the circle place all the words that you have decided upon.

Over a period of time people will put in and take out words as they begin to formulate the picture in their heads. Once the words are cemented in the middle of the circle and have not changed for a number of days you have your agreed values.

The next stage is to think – how can we put this together – what will our setting/school look like physically and feel like emotionally, what will the curriculum we offer entail, and what opportunities for deep-level application are we affording the children?

It is a very exciting and purposeful process to go through. Your vision and values are clear for all to see – this is what we aim for here and this is how we achieve it. If you are clear, concise and passionate others will buy into it.

Something to ponder upon...

If adults view energetic, action-orientated activity as immature and disruptive, and ask boys to conform to behaviours that they are not cognitively, physically or emotionally ready for this can lead to seeds of male underachievement in education being sown before the age of five.

Ask yourself these three simple questions:

1. What messages are we giving boys about their competence as learners?
2. To what extent do we value their natural drive and physicality?
3. Are we using their interests as starting points for learning journeys?

About this book

This book explores the different learning styles of boys, the competitive, visual and physical aspects of young male play and learning. It looks at why boys do what they do. It focuses on the different learning patterns of males and stresses that although there may be broad patterns of development that may be attributed to most children – the unique child must remain a central tenet for all practitioners. Not all boys do the same thing or indeed like the same thing.

The focus of the book is on the wider aspects of learning, what constitutes good learning and what practitioners need to provide in order to let children realise their full potential and to support areas that are in need of development.

The book discusses cognitive and physical development – how the brain works, the chemical make-up of male learners and how practitioners must provide an enabling environment, real stimulation and genuine empathy towards male learners, so that they see themselves as capable learners. It develops the themes of problem solving, risk taking and open-ended learning and considers how these might look in the development of a meaningful curriculum and learning experiences for young male learners.

The book explores the development of language and autonomy within boys, through useful stories, open-ended questions and sustained shared thinking. It looks at ways to ensure that boys are not 'overloaded' with too much information when undertaking challenges.

I also question the concept of learning – what does good learning look like and how is it measured? Is it through attainment and achievement or through positive dispositions and a willingness to learn about learning and think about thinking? The book considers how a

Getting it right for boys

positive disposition can be measured, certainly not via a test or wide-ranging nefarious statements at the end of the Foundation Stage.

It is well known that girls are out-performing boys in the early years, especially in PSE and literacy. Targets for local authorities have been based around the percentage of children achieving 78 points across the 13 aspects of the Early Years Foundation Stage Profile (2008) and 6+ points for PSE and literacy. Such a summative system takes little or no account of developmental or gender differences and in many cases forces practitioners into a 'check and assess' mentality rather than proper teaching and laying down a passion for learning through supporting children's natural inquisitiveness.

It is incredible that although it is well documented that boys develop physically and cognitively later than girls, in some instances up to 12–18 months later, the same assessment criteria applies. If one takes a summer born boy and an autumn born girl in the same class – chronologically there may be 11 months between them, but develop-mentally that could be up to two years – where is the fairness in assessing them against the same criteria?

Knowledgeable practitioners will, and should, argue that it is about the development the child makes from a given starting point that gives a great indication. Too few practitioners are doing this, however, and instead are utilising summative data to come to the wrong conclusions. In other words – boys are underachieving, let's do more of the same. The narrowness of the assessment procedure can have devastating effects and can label children as underachieving at the age of five. Figures for the 20 per cent lowest achieving children reveal that over 65 per cent are boys – the question is simple – WHY?

There desperately needs to be a focus on language development and how to engage boys in meaningful reflection, evaluation and planning of learning. We need to stimulate them to want to learn, to realise that learning is not about the 'boffins' or the 'geeks', and that ignorance is not cool. Learning should be happening all the time, it is a matter for adults to discover what, where, when and how.

This book covers practical ways to engage with young learners and suggests lines of enquiry that link to the needs and fascinations of boys. It looks at the use of rigorous observation and assessment to ensure that planning and the physical/emotional environment is suitable for boy learners. There is a section on environmental audits, open-ended resources and the learning opportunities that they afford children over a longer period of time.

The role of the adult is explored in depth – the need to recognise learning styles, needs and indeed where the learning is taking place and in what form the learning is developing.

There are case studies (little tales) of parents and practitioners who work with young boys, showing the successes and methodologies of true engagement in the learning process. Examples of templates to foster discussion between team members are included, using the *I am... I need... How as an adult do I ensure children receive it*, concept.

The main emphasis of this book is to put the child at the centre of learning and the 'fun' back into boys' learning. Learning will be taking place, albeit in a different guise, and it is the responsibility of the adult to identify and support it.

Overview of chapters

Chapter 1: What is the nature of a boy? This chapter looks at physical and cognitive development, language development, concentration and motivation.

Chapter 2: Why are boys underachieving? This chapter discusses what is meant by achievement – is it measurable? It considers the disposition to become a life-long learner.

Chapter 3: The role of the adult. This chapter recognises the need for sensitivity and stimulation, enabling learning to take place. It looks at how practitioners might embrace popular culture in the setting and how to be accepting of all children.

Chapter 4: The physical and emotional environment. This chapter looks at what makes a good learning environment and considers what is really meant by the term emotional well-being.

Chapter 5: Case studies. This chapter provides case studies which show what works for boys. It covers superhero and weapon play and looks at what the boys are actually learning through this play.

1 What is the nature of a boy?

Children's perceptions of each other

Girls think they are cleverer, more successful and harder working than boys from as young as four, according to a recent study. This is frightening news and is due to inappropriate learning and teaching strategies allied to low expectations, which results in a self-fulfilling prophesy.

The study, *Children's Development of Stereotypical Gender-related Expectations about Academic Engagement and Consequences for Performance*, carried out by the University of Kent, was presented to the British Educational Research Association annual conference at Warwick University in September 2010. The study presented 238 pupils aged four to ten with a series of statements such as 'this child is really clever' and 'this child always finishes their work' and asked them to link the words to pictures of boys or girls.

It emerged that girls at all ages said girls were cleverer, performed better and were more focused. Boys aged between four and seven were evenly divided as to which gender was cleverer and more hardworking. However by the time boys reached seven or eight, they agreed with their female peers that girls were more likely to be cleverer and more successful.

In a separate experiment, 140 of the children were divided into two groups. The researchers told the first group that boys do not perform as well as girls. The second group were not told this. All the pupils were tested in maths, reading and writing. The academics found the boys in the first group performed 'significantly worse' than boys in the second group, while the girls' performance was similar in both groups.

The paper argued that teachers and practitioners have lower expectations of boys than of girls and this belief fulfils itself throughout primary and secondary school. It claims that girls' performance at school may be boosted by what they perceive to be their teachers' belief that they will achieve higher results and be more conscientious than boys. Boys may underachieve because they pick up on teachers' assumptions that they will obtain lower results than girls and have less drive.

This research follows the publication of figures showing that boys are falling behind girls at the age of seven with 24 per cent of boys in England failing to reach the standard expected of their age group in writing compared with just 13 per cent of girls. This is even lower in the Foundation Stage where the gap between the genders continues to grow.

Messages of success and failure

The key question is where do children pick up these messages of success and failure? What has happened to a young child that they see themselves as somebody who will not achieve well? Without doubt, adults either consciously or unwittingly contribute to this 'self-fulfilling prophecy' by dividing and comparing classes into boys versus girls or using stereotypical language.

It is widely acceptable to pitch the boys against the girls or harmlessly divide the class in this way for practical ease. In addition, phrases such as 'silly boys', 'schoolboy pranks', 'mummy's little soldier', 'brave boys' and 'why can't you sit nicely like the girls?' are all likely to contribute to the expectation that boys not only behave worse and under-perform compared to girls, but should also be stoic and 'brave' about the process. This is when they are, in fact, desperate for support and comfort.

Phrases such as these tend to slip off the tongue, yet they may do more harm than is realised in reinforcing children's perceptions that it is acceptable to judge and evaluate people on the basis of their gender.

Male identities

Although the research is ten years old, *Boys' and Young Men's Health* (2001), a report on what '1400 boys really think about life in Britain at the turn of the century', is still relevant and the ensuing ten years has done little to assuage the identity crisis brought about by changing gender roles and expectations.

According to *Leading Lads*, a project conducted in association with Oxford University and sponsored by Top Man, the young male population can be split into three categories: 'can-do boys' (optimistic, confident and motivated); 'average' boys and 'low can-do boys' (isolated, unmotivated and sometimes depressed). The report shows that as boys get older they have more chance of slipping into the 'low can-do' category. Only six per cent of 13-year-old boys are 'low can-do' compared to a whopping 27 per cent of 19-year-olds.

There is little doubt that societal expectations of what it means to be a 'man' have changed over the decades. But have perceptions of 'manhood' changed in the classroom or the early years setting? What do practitioners expect of boys, what do they expect them to achieve, to be like, to behave like and how are they assisting or otherwise in this process?

A little tale – here's Jimmy (age four)

This is my day (Part one) – every day

'I like running, it is my best thing, I am really good at running, I think I am the fastest runner. Sometimes I run all the way to school, mummy chases me, it's funny. I don't fall over any more, I did when I was little, but I am big now so I don't do that anymore. I like running fast with my friends so we catch the baddies and put them in the jail. We play police and I say 'stop' to the baddies. I got a police hat and jacket. At school I can't run and have to walk, it's so slow. Sometimes I get told off for running and have to sit on the 'thinking chair', it's too hard.

I like playing with the train set, I've got one at home with Thomas and Henry and Gordon and James... sometimes the train is out and I can play with it and share with my friend, that's good that is, my best story is when Henry gets stuck in the tunnel because it's raining, he's so silly. But sometimes the train is in the box at school and I can't get it out so I don't have anything to play with.'

Camping – a male odyssey

A couple of summers ago a group of friends invited me and a colleague to join them in a weekend's camping expedition on the wilds of Dartmoor. These were seasoned and professional campers who had been partaking in this particular brand of male bonding for some considerable time. The organisation was akin to a military expedition, well planned, clear departure and arrival points, meal times, storage, fire building requirements, waste disposal – it was all very impressive.

They had all the gear, all the accessories, fanciful gadgets, high quality tents and sleeping equipment. They knew how it was done and the best and quickest way to do it. They would not, for example, try to inflate the mattress just before they were about to go to bed, having had a few beers – it does not work and results in a very uncomfortable night! They knew what was important to do first prior to relaxing, putting things in order – a linear way of progressing, first we do this, then that, then...

Each member of the team was given responsibilities and undertook these with complete control and confidence. Why? It was because they knew what to do and how to do it, working within the strengths of the team. We, on the other hand, were relative novices to this high-end camping. Our equipment was inferior (especially our chairs that did not have arms on them!), we bought bottles as opposed to squashable tins, our eating utensils were not up to standard and our tent-raising skills were on the amateurish side. In short, we knew our place, we were at the bottom of the chain, and we could bring nothing to the event save our gracious good company – so for the first night we watched and learnt.

A key requirement to the weekend was, of course, maintaining a steady fire which, in turn, needed a steady supply of combustible wood material. The agreement was simple: when you disappeared into the woods for ablutions you came back with some fire wood and added to the ever-increasing stock pile.

It was here that the first unspoken challenge was laid down to the group – someone went to the woods and returned brandishing a slightly larger item of wood and quietly placed it on the log pile – the challenge was on. How would people react to this challenge? Nothing was said, but there was a tacit understanding that larger bits of wood were required when you returned from the woods. From that point on people were returning with ever-increasing sizes of wood and having to travel ever-greater distances down precarious paths and slopes to retrieve them.

As time progressed it became apparent that the wood that was being returned was simply getting too large for the lone individual to haul back by themselves – the solution – team up. So not only was there individual challenge, but this had transformed into a team challenge. Who would work with whom? What was the best technique for bringing wood back? Where was the best wood to be found?

This in essence is the very nature of a boy: competitive, looking for a challenge, cooperative and visual in learning style – watching, noting, responding, doing and retrospective problem solving. The interesting thing here is that as grown men we were acting and reacting in much the same way as young children, nothing in the intervening period between childhood and adulthood has fundamentally changed; the reactions and thinking processes remain the same.

One of the overriding reasons for this way of being is the preponderance of testosterone in boys' chemical make-up and the impact this has on well-being and needs.

Testosterone – the legacy on learning

Testosterone has two different kinds of effects. One effect is anabolic. This effect causes growth of muscle and bone. The other effect of testosterone is androgenic.

Testosterone is the most important sex hormone (otherwise known as androgen) produced in the male body. It is the hormone that is primarily responsible for producing and maintaining the typical adult male attributes. At puberty, testosterone stimulates the physical changes that characterise the adult male, such as enlargement of the penis and testes, growth of facial and pubic hair, deepening of the voice, an increase in muscle mass and strength, and growth in height.

Throughout adult life, testosterone helps maintain sex drive, the production of sperm cells, male hair patterns, muscle mass and bone mass. Testosterone is produced mostly in the testes and a small amount of testosterone is produced from steroids secreted by the outer layer of the adrenal glands (called the adrenal cortex). In females, small amounts of testosterone are produced by the ovaries.

While it is commonly perceived that testosterone is not a major factor in prepubescent male development, testosterone is active long before puberty begins. For example, while a fetus is still in the womb, testosterone and a product of its metabolism, dihydrotestosterone, cause the male genitalia to form.

Testosterone is a hormone with quite a personality. As the primary male sex hormone produced by the testicles, testosterone tends to be identified with all we stereotype as masculine.

How much of our behaviour is controlled by the biology of our hormones? Does testosterone really make the man? It's a debate that's been waged in scientific and social circles for decades. Some have attributed high levels of testosterone to criminal tendencies while others call it the hormone of desire.

Testosterone in men and women

Despite popular belief, testosterone is a many-gendered hormone. It belongs in the hormonal kitbags of both men and women, and can play a role in the well-being of us all – male, female... or anywhere in between. Nevertheless testosterone should perhaps be best known as the 'value-laden hormone', caught in a confusing web of social expectations and gender stereotypes.

Testosterone is one of a family of hormones called androgens. Best known for their masculinising effects, androgens first kick into action during the embryonic stages of life. To explain, let's go back to the basics of reproduction biology. An embryo is conceived when a female egg is fertilised with a male sperm. The egg and sperm each donate a single sex chromosome to the embryo, an X chromosome from women, and an X or Y chromosome from men.

Getting it right for boys

If the combination of these sex chromosomes is XX, then the embryo will be female. If it's XY, the embryo will be male. Though in fact, it's not until the sixth week of development that XX or XY embryos are anatomically defined. Before this the human foetus is essentially sexless, possessing a set of 'indifferent' genitalia. One interpretation of this is that all embryos begin as female. Testosterone makes the difference, influencing the growth of male genitalia while the female component of the indifferent genitalia degenerates. But is it only the absence of foetal testosterone that causes an embryo to develop in a female direction? It's a question that we know less about.

According to some, the intimate association between testosterone and male identity starts this early. Anne Fausto-Sterling, in her book, *Myths of Gender* (1992), believes this inference that 'testosterone equals male', while 'absence of testosterone equals female', is well-entrenched in the layers of our culture as a notion of 'female as lack', and that 'such rock-bottom cultural ideas can intrude unnoticed even into the scientist's laboratory'.

Testosterone is also well known for its role in the hormonal hotbed that is male puberty. As well as these androgenic or masculinising effects, testosterone also drives anabolic or tissue-building changes. These include thickening of the vocal chords, growth spurts, development of sexual libido, and an increase in strength and muscle bulk.

There's no denying these powerful physical effects which continue well into adulthood, and their driving force – hormones. But we feel compelled to box our hormones resolutely into those that belong to men, or to women. Estrogen and progesterone are the so-called female sex hormones, and testosterone, the so-called primary male sex hormone. With that we assign our hormones impossible gender roles. But of course gender is not that simple, and nor are our hormones.

It turns out men and women produce exactly the same hormones, only in different amounts. Men's bodies generate more than 20 times more testosterone than women, an average of seven milligrams per day. Women, via mainly their ovaries and adrenal glands, make a tiny three tenths of one milligram of testosterone per day. But it may come as a surprise to know that women's ovaries primarily produce testosterone, from which estrogen is then made. This ovarian production accounts for one-quarter of the total circulating testosterone in a woman's body. Conversely, men's bodies produce their own all-womanly estrogen, converted by their tissues from their all-manly testosterone.

It's not surprising that our levels of testosterone are understood to affect our behaviour. Testosterone receptors are found in our brain, which means the hormone interacts and binds with our neurons, relaying to them important messages for action.

Testosterone in boys and young men

Young boys are rife with testosterone, they are hit with a rush around the ages of two to three and again around seven, prior to the onset of puberty around 12 to 13. This final onset is not only physically life-altering as the voice deepens and hairs start to sprout in the oddest of places, muscle starts to be laid down, bones expand and joints weaken, it is also cognitively life-altering as confusion, anger and unfairness are key emotions and a sense of identity is being formed.

This life-altering state for young men can be traumatic and confusing – suddenly they start to fancy the girls in the class, but physically they do not look their best, their trousers are too short, they get spots, greasy hair, 'bum fluff beards', squeaky and deep voices at the same time. They ache and they are tired.

The same emotions are there for the youngest of learners, something is happening to them, but they don't know what it is and don't have the necessary vocabulary or emotional cognitiveness to express it. They get frustrated and angry, yet still need a cuddle and reassurance!

Testosterone, generally, makes boys (and some girls) energetic, boisterous and competitive. There is a need for hierarchy, and this is manifested in physical play, rough and tumble and physical contact. There is a great need for self-confidence, self-reliance, and problem-solving, risk-taking activities.

There is a great deal of single-mindedness, a real need to be recognised, valued, and managed. As a result boys need stimulation, variety and physical activity. They also love HUMOUR.

The learning environment

Generally boys have more testosterone pumping about their bodies. This makes them competitive, action orientated and excitable. Generally girls will have a lower level of testosterone and will therefore be more compliant, settled and less excitable. I must add here that 'compliance' does not equate to obedience or lack of imagination but rather that girls will 'get on' and start to organise themselves and their play earlier and in more detail than the boys.

It's well worth looking at the way the boys in your schools and settings are interacting with the environment:

- Where is the learning happening?
- What is the nature of the learning?
- How are they learning? Do I allow this style to happen or does it cut across my own vision of 'good learning'? There does seem to be a deeply entrenched view within many schools and settings that 'good learning' happens when children are quiet and sitting down, not when they are active, lying down, rolling around or running.
- Are there places that the boys prefer? Why is this?
- Are there places the boys avoid? Why is this?

We shall return to this self-reflection and detailed analysis later in this chapter.

Boys' brains and girls' brains

Even in the most 'meaningful' and 'enlightened' households where families actively encourage their boys to cuddle dolls and examine the 'sensitive' side of life, most boys will take to Thomas the Tank Engine, Ben 10 and superhero play rather than ponies and dolls.

Undoubtedly some of this behaviour is learned, but the gap between boys and girls goes far deeper than upbringing and nurture. It is suspected that even before birth boys' and girls' brains are developing differently and consequently turning them into different little people.

So is there such a thing as a boy brain and a girl brain? Yes. We know there are physical differences between a boy's brain and a girl's, both at birth and as children grow. But at least for now, exactly how those differences affect behaviour, personality, and so on is a mystery. For example, scientists say there probably is an area of the brain that propels many boys toward things that move and many girls toward nurturing and the emotional side of learning, but it has yet to be identified.

Leonard Sax's work with newborn infants has highlighted this. On one side of the cot he would have a moving object and on the other side parents would be looking at the child. He carried this out on both sides of the cot to ensure consistency. He found that in the vast majority of cases the boys would look towards the moving object while the girls would look at the faces of the doting parents. So even from birth children's brains are wired differently and interested in different things.

Men on the whole are poor at reading the non-verbal signs of communication – I have found this to be true many times. As a male in early years I am usually working with a predominantly female workforce. On numerous occasions I have been accused of 'lack of tact and understanding' as I do not read the subliminal messages that may manifest themselves in a look or a glance.

'Didn't you see the look?' is a question I am often asked – the reply is almost always 'What look?' It is not that I am an insensitive soul, or at least hope I am not, it is just that my brain does not necessarily work in the same way – and prefers to be told outright rather than 'guess' people's emotional responses to situations.

Brain development in the womb

So how does a boy's brain develop in the womb? Boys in the womb are little testosterone machines. In fact, says Margaret M. McCarthy (2007), a professor of physiology at the University of Maryland who studies early brain development, male babies are born with as much testosterone as a 25-year-old man. Think about the impact all that testosterone, raging through young bodies has on your physical and emotional environments! Amongst its many other jobs, testosterone shapes a male's developing brain by paring down the connections between brain cells (synapses) in some places and bulking them up in other places. There is some evidence that high levels of testosterone improve spatial reasoning.

How does a girl's brain develop in the womb? Berenbaum (2006) explains that girls make some testosterone before they're born, too, but not nearly as much as boys. And while girls do produce female hormones such as estrogen, these seem to have little impact on their developing brains.

Brain development of children

Once girls and boys are born, their brains continue to take different paths. MRI studies show that some areas grow faster in female brains while others grow faster in male brains. So, the brains of boys and girls who are the same age can be at different developmental stages. It is crucial that this is recognised by early years practitioners so that expectation is correctly differentiated. Not all the children will be able to do the same thing at the same time and it is vital that early years practitioners are well schooled in developmental issues. Eventually, though, boys and girls can catch up with each other.

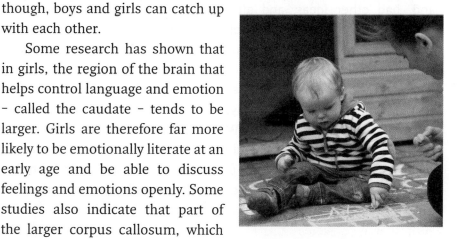

Some research has shown that in girls, the region of the brain that helps control language and emotion – called the caudate – tends to be larger. Girls are therefore far more likely to be emotionally literate at an early age and be able to discuss feelings and emotions openly. Some studies also indicate that part of the larger corpus callosum, which connects the two sides of the brain, is larger in girls than in boys. Some scientists think this could mean that girls tend to use both the left and right sides to solve problems.

Girls use up to 30 times more language in their play than boys. This language disparity leads to differences in social and emotional development between the genders.

If you take the opportunity to observe children at play, and I strongly urge that you do this, you will note where the learning happens, what learning happens, who learns in certain ways, the language used and the emotional and social relationships being formed. Generally girls are far more adept at 'getting on' – emotionally they are further developed than their male peers and consequently use words and social interactions to organise, clarify and think about thinking.

Boys on the other hand, due to lack of language and emotional development, will use action and often solitary play to organise, clarify and think about thinking. Are you allowing this to happen in your setting?

A little tale – here's Jack (age six)

I observed Jack playing with one of his good friends, a young girl. Jack was full of ideas but lacked the required vocabulary and social interactions to put his well-meaning but rather random ideas into practice. It was his intention to be the leader in this little game. His friend, on the other hand, had other ideas, and after being incredibly patient to Jack's wayward ramblings took control of the situation and started to tell Jack exactly what they were going to do and how they were going to do it.

After listening for a minute or two Jack's concentration span had come to an end. In exasperation he looked skyward and shouted, 'You are always talking, talk talk, talk, always talking at me (a very observant little boy 'at' is key) all I hear is talk!' With that he promptly reverted to boy behaviour and punched his friend on the arm and ran away to put his thoughts into action – which were pure genius – to colour his little brother in using felt tips. Something he did and was incredibly proud of as well!

Physical contact

Boys love physical contact, it is reassurance that they are respected, loved and valued as part of a group. If one looks at those children who are distressed on arrival at nurseries and pre-schools one will find that the large majority are young boys. Breaking that physical attachment is very difficult – boys love a cuddle and a hug. From my own experience with our youngest – who is now big and on his own adventures – he was a nightmare when it came to sleeping on his own as a young child. He could not be left alone and would constantly wail, scream and cry as though it was the end of the world. It was physically and emotionally draining.

So for sanity and sleep we put him in our bed – not condoning or precluding such an action – but for sanity's sake it was something that just had to be done. Of course he was then an extremely happy bunny, cuddling up, snuggling and – hooray – sleeping through the night. The draw-back though, he never wanted to leave!

It brought home to me how young males attach themselves, how much physical contact they love – you may well have young boys in your setting who cling onto legs and hands as though their very existence depended on it. Watch this in their play, the rough and tumble, the very physical nature of relationships. Good practitioners understand this play and actively engage in it, for it is how boys gain a sense of self, a sense of purpose and a sense of identity within a group.

Watching older males is also fascinating – the amount of physical contact is staggering. Back-rubbing, hand-shaking, arms around shoulders. It is saying '*We are alright, we are friends, and I can rely on you as a good mate'*. There is no need for language, for a discussion on emotions, a hug and an embrace makes everything alright.

So far we have looked predominantly at the role testosterone plays in a boy's nature and make up – there are however a multitude of other chemicals, hormones, physical and cognitive issues that need to be uncovered.

How serotonin affects the ways that boys learn

Serotonin is a well-known contributor to feelings of well-being and it is also known to contribute to happiness. Boys produce less of this in their bodies; they also have less oxytocin, the primary human bonding chemical. This makes it more likely that they will be physically impulsive and less likely that they will neurally combat their natural impulsiveness and sit still and empathically chat with a friend, Moir and Jessel (1980); Taylor (2002).

The result of this is that boys are more compulsive, non-cautious, eager and liable to take risks. Girls on the other hand are more controlled, logical and analytical. Girls often take a strategic view and plan for consequences, they see issues before they arise and use their greater reasoning and language capacity to plan appropriate plans of action. They can see the links – if we do this, then this will happen. This does not specifically apply to boys, where there is a more *gung ho* approach to events – let's do it, modify as we go along and adjust at the end.

Take the analogy of the flat-packed *Ikea* shelves. Many men will empty the box, take a rudimentary look at the abstract diagram, promptly discard it and set about putting the items together by looking at what piece they believe fits into another. It is this primeval drive to get on with it and be hands-on that practitioners need to be aware of and encourage. Practitioners can support this way of working through open-ended questioning, modelling language and letting children explain their thinking processes.

Boys will often not see the risk until after the event. This is retrospective analysis of a problem and boys will need to act out the problem in concrete terms in order to adjust and modify their thinking. The abstract analysis is not yet developed enough. Boys very much learn by doing, it is the doing that is creative and in the doing comes the evaluation. Sensitive adult stimulation and open-ended discussion will support boys in the thinking process.

It is vital that such evaluation does not become adult dominated – I have heard *'I don't think that's a good idea. Do you?'* so often. Wouldn't it be lovely if they could say back, *'Well yes I do think it's a good idea, that's why I am doing it, so please stop being so negative about everything! And let me get on with it and find out loads of stuff – THANK YOU VERY MUCH!'*

Let's look at this from the perspective of a couple of four-year-old boys.

Getting it right for boys

A little tale – here are Shaheen and Michael

Shaheen and Michael are on a mission, they are outside in the garden meaningfully engaged in a child-initiated project. They need to get the roofing on the house all sorted out in case it starts to rain. Michael has been busy telling Shaheen how his dad is a 'roofer and has to go up big ladders putting things on roofs to stop the rain coming in'. However, there are a few problems to circumvent; firstly what shall they use for roofing materials, secondly how shall they transport them to the house and thirdly how shall they get them up on the roof?

After a lengthy discussion, well, all of a minute, but that is pretty lengthy for this intrepid duo of roofing specialists, they decide upon the Community Plaything blocks – all different shapes and sizes and just ideal for the job in hand. The next problem is how are they going to transport all these blocks to the house?

Initially they try carrying them, but soon get fed up as it is taking 'just too long'. A new strategy is required. Shaheen suggests that they use the wheelbarrow to take the blocks – an excellent suggestion. They then concentrate in loading up the barrow with blocks, not too many so that they can't push it and not too few that it takes ages to transport. This is a deep-thinking process, 'It's too heavy, I'll have to empty some out' says Michael as he struggles manfully across the playground.

Eventually all the blocks are over by the house. Now comes problem number three, just how are they going to get the blocks up on the roof? 'We can use the ladders' says Michael, and promptly goes to the shed to retrieve the required items. This again is heavy work as the boys carry the ladder over to the house and prop it up.

Michael climbs the ladder and Shaheen passes up the blocks – the work has begun. The boys spend the entire morning 'tiling' the roof.

More than anything else what had supported this in-depth learning and application of knowledge was a sensitive adult who supported the choices made by the boys, allowed them to make their own decisions and problem solve issues themselves without taking over the play or being in any way dominant.

One only has to visit *YouTube* and watch people doing daft things, to see how boys learn best, to see how the lack of serotonin requires a more direct hands-on approach to learning. A quick look will tell you that the majority of 'stunts' and 'crazy schemes' are cooked up by young males – full of hormones, competing against themselves and others.

If you look back at the Early Years Foundation Stage Profile (2008) statements regarding 'motivation and interested in learning' this is exactly what is happening here – albeit in a less than censored way. If you sit and think for a moment of the creativity, problem solving, modification and risk taking that has taken place in order to perform one of these 'stunts' – then real learning has taken place. An idea has been thought out, analysed, a problem solved and modified. If you are to look at 'What makes a good principle', it is here in droves – the success criteria have been set and the methodology to acquire the said result is in place.

How dopamine affects the ways boys learn

In girls, the language areas of the brain develop before the areas used for spatial relations and geometry. In boys, it's the other way around. A curriculum which ignores these differences will produce boys who can't write and girls who think they're 'rubbish at maths'.

In girls, emotion is processed in the same area of the brain that processes language. So, it's not too difficult for most girls to talk about their emotions. In boys, the brain regions involved in talking are separate from the regions involved in feeling.

The typical teenage girl has a sense of hearing which is significantly better than a teenage boy. That's why daughters so often complain that their fathers are shouting at them. Girls in general have more dopamine, so they hear better, listen more attentively and are in need of less stimulation. Boys conversely have less dopamine; they have shorter attention spans, and are in need of greater stimulation.

It is well recorded that boys hear less than girls – research suggests that they hear 70 per cent less from birth, and here's the rub, it doesn't get any better! This is all down to the RAS (Reticular Activating System) in the brain. The RAS is a part of your brain that filters information. Your brain is continually bombarded with thousands of pieces of information. If you consciously took note of them all, you would experience brain overload. It will only let information through that is directly relevant or of interest to us as individuals.

You might have experienced this yourself if you've ever asked a male partner to complete a few jobs while you are out:

'Can you empty the washing machine, hang it out and get the books out of the bedroom and pop them in a box for the jumble sale?' The immediate response will be *'OK leave it to me'.* However, realistically, what are the chances that all four requests will have been carried out by your return? Pretty slim I would suggest, pretty slim indeed. Then comes the old chestnut, *'Well, I can't be expected to remember everything can I – I have other things to do as well you know'.* This is followed by walking out of the room in a huff, and perhaps the slamming of a door or two in the process. Just wonderful!

I remember trying to get my son to have a rudimentary attempt at tidying up his room and put a few things away. It soon transpired that the whole concept of tidying the room was just too big   where do you start? Oh it is just so confusing! The best strategy was to do one thing at a time and I mean literally one thing at a time – starting with *'Let's open the drawers'.* Ah ha, the drawers yes I can do that. *'Now pick up your socks',* right got them, still with it, *'Now put the socks IN the drawer'* – still with you dad – good work!

We need to be very conscious of the amount of information we give to boys, too often we overload them with information and questions, and their brains will not take it on board. A very useful reflective exercise is to ask one of your colleagues to shadow you when you are interacting with children and ask them to note down every time you ask a question and the amount of information you give.

A good rule of thumb is one question to every four statements. Statements here are a commentary of children's learning, *'Oh I see that you are... I like the way that... That's interesting how...'*

Far too often when I am in schools and settings I hear what I term as the 'Trinity of questions' – I think you know what they are – but just in case here's a little story. I have placed myself as a child in this one just in case you are thinking 'How does he know what they are thinking?'

I am playing with the play dough with Ahmed and Jordan. Today the play dough is green. We are making worms and big snakes. Jordan likes snakes, he says he has three at his house, and he showed photos of them, they look all slippery to me. We are having lots of fun talking about snakes and what they eat. I have rolled a big long one, and it's so long it's falling off the table. Jordan is making a bigger one, wow, Ahmed's snake is really fat, it's funny, and he says it's fat because it has eaten all the other snakes.

Oh no! Here comes a grown-up – we know what she's going to say, she always says the same thing! We laugh. Ahmed says 'I bet she says what colour are the snakes first?' Jordan says 'No way, she's going to ask how many snakes have we made?' I say that I think she's going to say 'What shape are the snakes?'

We wait, here she comes, we are laughing now, really giggling, she sits down and says, 'How many snakes have got?' We erupt, 'How many snakes? Well, there are ten and they are green and they are mostly cylindrical, now please leave us alone so we can carry on playing!'

If only they would do this – it would be a revelation to adults!

A little tale – here's Jimmy (remember him?)

This is my day (Part two) – every day

'It's lunchtime and Jimmy has had a busy and exhausting morning trying not to run about chasing the baddies and putting them in jail. The train set wasn't out today so Jimmy found it difficult to settle into any learning and retell his favourite stories; it hasn't been the best of mornings.

Jimmy is looking forward to lunch so he can run about in the big playground and perhaps catch those pesky baddies. He is sitting down on the carpet, it's a bit boring and he is fidgeting with his shoe, he just can't get comfortable. Suddenly the grown-up asks Jimmy to get his coat, put it on and on the way back pick up the marbles, put them in the drawer and put the lids on the pens in the writing area. Jimmy knows he's in trouble, he knows he won't be able to remember all that stuff, but he's been told he is a big boy now.

Jimmy gets up and walks over to the coats. He stops. He can't remember what else he was supposed to do. He panics and stands by the coats fiddling with his hood, he really isn't very good at putting his coat on, sometimes it's alright but other times it's inside out and back to front. The grown-up isn't looking now, Jimmy really cannot remember all the other things he was supposed to do so he drops his coat on the floor and quickly and quietly scampers back to the carpet – not a happy bunny at all.'

The key point here is that with young boys, well in fact most men if truth be told, you will need to *chunk out learning*. Make it short and concise so that boys know the next step in the sequence and are not overloaded with too much superfluous information. By doing this you will be meeting the needs of the children, giving them confidence and allowing them to develop their own learning journeys.

To ensure that you are interacting with the RAS make sure that:

- resources and activities are of interest. Boys in particular love weird and interesting stuff – stuff to take apart to explore, old radios, backs of TVs, keyboards, non-fiction books and comics. They like big things to physically explore.
- materials are age-appropriate and challenging. This is an interesting point as far too often resources are just put out as table-fillers. Planning results in activity rather than being learning-based. Think about your resources. What are you expecting the children to do with them? Children have the same construction bricks in the toddler room, the nursery and in the reception class. What is the differentiation and what is the purpose of putting them out?
- your environment is linked to observations, assessment and planning.
- you build on prior learning and experiences to meet individual learning needs.

The emotional brain

This is also known as the limbic brain. This part has memory. It also maintains blood pressure, heart rate and body temperature. It is critical to learning and for short and long term memory. It stores memories of your lifetime.

The limbic brain responds to the five senses. As a child of the late sixties 'multi-sensory learning' was something that I grew up with and was surrounded by. Sensory experiences are vital for children's long-term memory. Learning is more effective when an experience is linked to one of the senses or an emotion so ensure that your enabled environment provides a range of sensory experiences. The environment needs to:

- smell nice
- look nice
- have the right space
- have interesting things to feel
- have tasty things to eat.

It is important that these aspects are in place if a young male learner is to succeed. This part of the brain stores all the emotional baggage – did I enjoy my early days or did I not?

Think of yourself here – you have had a bad day, the children's rooms are a tip, the washing is not on the line despite promises that it would be, the *Ikea* shelf is falling down and there are a couple of dozen spare screws lurking about in the box. You are just thoroughly cheesed off with the whole thing.

Then on the radio – it's The Human League's 'Don't You Want Me Baby' (showing my age here) – happy days! You are transported back to 1981, snoods, leg warmers, ridiculous hair-cuts, shoulder pads, eye liner and androgynous young men. It is a different time and place when things were OK with the world. Immediately you are in a 'nice' place, your emotions calm down and you reassert calmness.

This is how the limbic brain works – in the long term we as early years practitioners want to store up in children's minds as many positive memories as we can. We want all children, and in particular boys, to have a positive recollection of their early years, a can-do attitude based upon good memories and positive experiences.

So it is well worth asking of your setting – does it elicit a positive emotional response? Do my routines and resources allow emotional connectivity with the learning experience? And if not – how can I change it?

One of the main reasons why some parents do not interact with schools is not that they are uninterested in their child's education, but because the school or settings bring back unhappy memories and there is an immediate cut-off. It is therefore crucial that your setting/school is visually pleasing, smells nice (a good old-fashioned toast bar works wonders here, who doesn't like the smell of toast?), has interesting things to taste and feel and a noise level that is calm and busy.

If you put yourself in the place of a child, what does your setting 'feel' like? It might be that you have to get on your hands and knees and crawl around the floor to get a child's perspective of your setting. What does it look and feel like from down here?

You need to ask yourself – *'Would I like to come here? Is this space meeting my emotional, physical, and cognitive needs?'* Ask yourself why you like to go to certain shops or places. What are the underlying reasons that you return to these spaces – do they meet your needs and if so, how? Is it the resources, the smells, the attentive staff or how the displays are organised?

In essence, your setting and school is a shop for children, and in this case boys, where they can pick and mix the learning because it is so rich in learning choices and excitement. It should be based upon them and their fascinations, their interests. They are an active part of the process in developing the learning and the learning environment.

An interesting characteristic of the limbic brain is that it loves to know it's doing a good job and to know it can do even better. Positive praise is crucial – but this praise cannot be unconditional, it needs to be merited and worthwhile. In many settings there is too low an expectation on young male learners. Random praise is handed out that has no meaning *'Oh look at you, well done for breathing, have a sticker'.* Praise needs to be differentiated by expectation, and expectation is garnered through an in-depth knowledge of the individual child – what are their strengths, how do they learn, what are the areas for development?

Children are smart little cookies and soon latch onto the fact that expectations are low and will play to that denominator. If we truly want our boys to achieve well in later years then praise must be chanelled correctly.

Physical and cognitive development

Here are some fascinating facts, which should have an impact on your provision, resources and routines. Boys' ankles and wrists are not fully developed until they are around five and a half to six years old – the thumb and the metacarpal, even later. Girls develop a whole year or year and a half earlier!

It is a sad indictment of our modern and supposedly enlightened times that children are becoming more sedentary than ever before. It is now believed that the average five-year-old cannot do what three-year-olds were doing ten to twelve years ago. There are many reasons for this: a preponderance of push-chair kids, lack of challenging play space, overt health and safety officialdom curtailing any semblance of risk taking, and a dominance of the computer screen and video games. Children are less well physically rounded than before and the numbers of obese and overweight children seems to be rising each year.

We need to get children moving and a well-organised balance system indicates a well-organised brain. Balance is trained through movement. Those children who are unable to stay still are showing that their balance and motor systems are not yet sufficiently mature to remain still for long periods of time. They need to move to get their brains into gear.

The rule of thumb for how many minutes children can sit still for is their age plus two – I would suggest that for boys this is even shorter. Sitting still is the most advanced stage of physical development as you then have complete control over your body. You need to seriously ask yourself – how long do I expect children to be sitting still and more importantly why?

Children need to be physically comfortable in order to cognitively and emotionally engage with an experience. Making children sit for prolonged periods of time can soon turn even the most eager learner into a disaffected young soul. Two years ago I carried out research with six-year-old children about their favourite and least favourite parts of the school day in Year One. The findings were astonishing, and for boys in particular the least favourite time was 'story time', a part of the day that should be relaxing and fun. They did not like it because it involved prolonged periods of sitting down in uncomfortable positions listening to an adult. Is there any learning going on here?

You have to ask yourself what is the purpose of such routines, are they about learning and listening or are they about control? I have witnessed too many group and story times where the learning intention is lost because the adult is adamant that all children are sitting quietly with hands on laps and legs crossed. Boys in particular find this excruciating and such positions can cause physical discomfort, so there is no way on earth any deep-level enjoyment or learning will take place.

A little tale – here's Jimmy (remember him?)

This is my day (Part three) – every day

'It's carpet time. I don't like carpet time and we have to sit for ages. My legs hurt and I can't cross them all the way, but the grown-up says I have to. Sometimes I have to move and the grown-up tells me off, because I can't sit still. We have to come to the carpet after lunch and have a story. I would like to lie down. Robert always gets told off for moving around and so we sit for an even longer time.'

When you go home in the evening and get yourself ready to watch your favourite television programme or read the book you are engrossed in do you sit on the carpet with your legs crossed? The chances of doing this are pretty remote. You will probably get yourself a nice cup of tea, a few snacks, fluff up the cushions on the sofa and get yourself snug. You are now physically comfortable and emotionally secure so the experience will be a pleasurable one.

Does it matter if the children, and boys in particular, are lying down at story time, or standing up at a jaunty angle eating a banana? No, it

does not – children need to be comfortable, so please let it happen and relinquish some adult power here because the focus has to be children's involvement in the learning process. Otherwise the learning intention of any carpet session will be lost and the focus will be on *'waiting for children to be still and quiet'*. Invariably it will always be the same children who you are waiting for, so the learning is lost, the attention is lost and carpet time is equated to an unpleasant experience in the limbic brain.

Crossing the centre line

In order for children to become physically balanced individuals they need to cross the 'centre line', the line that runs down the middle of their bodies. Observations of children painting will tell you if this is happening, happened, or yet to happen. You might well note that children in your setting, when painting, will hold the brush in the left hand and paint to the middle of the paper; they then move the brush to the right hand and continue. The reason for this is very simple, they cannot yet make a line that carries them from one side of the paper to the other, and they have not crossed that middle line. The synapses in the brain have not yet connected.

A very useful exercise to assist children in crossing this middle line is the 'lazy 8'. A lazy 8 I hear you cry, what on earth is a lazy 8? Well it is exactly what it says it is, an 8 on its side.

This is a great little activity to assist children in getting across the middle line and can be carried out anywhere in your setting – on the finger-painting table, on big bits of paper, on the floor or on the wall. I used to have lazy 8 shapes all over my classrooms when I was teaching. On the wall I would have a large piece of paper, two foot prints at the centre of the 8 and some thick markers so the children could trace the shape. They would start in the middle and go up to the right, always keeping the pen on the paper or the finger in the paint so it was a single continuous movement. It is an incredibly therapeutic and relaxing activity and children would spend ages going over the 8 – constantly crossing that middle line.

You can also do this with children by standing in front of them and saying *'Follow my finger with your eyes and don't move your head'*. You would then start at the nose and draw a lazy 8 in the air to gauge whether children can follow the finger across both sides of the body. Some will be able to do this, others will have to refocus when you come back to the middle and will invariably start to follow your finger with their head, not their eyes. Children will not be able to read or write until they have crossed this middle line.

So if they cannot – *get them outside and climbing and balancing.*

Through your observations and knowledge of the children in your school/setting you may have picked up on what I term the 'bumbly' children. These children are almost always boys. You can spot them a mile away. They:

- cannot walk across the setting without touching surfaces on the way – they do this in order to anchor themselves in the space. To put it bluntly they do not know where they are, they do not know the extremities of their bodies or where they are in space.
- sit on children at group times or knock them out of the way at the sand and water trays – they literally cannot see them and calculate how their own body mass will fit into the space provided.

These boys require our help and urgently. Children are not dismissive by nature but you will find that these bumbly boys will become socially ostracised by their peers who do not want to be sat on or squashed so they move away. The affect this has on emotional well-being and self-image is devastating. They become the outsiders of the group, the solitary children, later to be found in the primary playground sitting on the 'friendship bench'. And to think that for many boys this is a daily occurrence in their formative pre-school and school years.

So when you are looking at provision and interactions, put yourself in the shoes of those young boys in your setting and ask:

- Do I have a positive self-image? No
- Do I have a close group of friends? No
- Do I enjoy myself and join in? No
- Do I feel lonely and awkward? Yes
- Do I like coming here? No

Bearing in mind that boys physically develop later than girls, it is imperative that we get them moving so that any developmental gap may be bridged, so that we have boys with a positive self-image, and a can-do feeling about themselves as capable, creative and confident learners.

A little tale - here's Jimmy again

This is my day (Part four) - every day

I observed Jimmy following a group 'letters and sounds' session. The group was learning about the letter 'j' and the sound that it makes as part of their phonics programme. The follow-up task, the exciting application (as it should be) was to sit at a table and write lots of 'j's. What this had to do with practical application of phonics in meaningful contexts is beyond me – but it was the activity on offer and Jimmy had to join his peers at the table sitting on a chair with a pencil and an A4 worksheet to copy the letter.

Jimmy found it incredibly difficult to sit comfortably at the table; he was a right fidget-bottom, moving about trying to get into a comfortable position. He also found it difficult to grasp the thin pencil in the correct manner and write on a small piece of paper. He was struggling. Jimmy sat at the table for 25 minutes and had written three plausible 'j's. His peers had all left, but Jimmy knew he had to cover the whole page, so he sat there watching his peers go about their learning choices.

Five minutes later Jimmy was still sitting there, well I mean sitting in its loosest possible meaning, he was in fact more hanging off the chair. His head was slumped on the table, one arm covering his attempt at 'j' writing, the other lolling limply by his side. I sidled up to Jimmy and enquired if he was alright. He turned and looked at me and said 'No I ain't, it's killing me, all this writing, it's killing my hands'. What more could I say apart from let's leave it and go and find something interesting to do.

It is well worth recapping on Jimmy's day at this juncture:

- I like to run, because I am so fast, but I can't.
- I love playing with the trains, but I can't because they are not out today.
- I get asked to do too many things and I can't remember all of them.
- I have to sit down with my legs crossed for a long time, this hurts you know.
- I have to sit at a table on a chair and write loads of letters – I can't do this very well and it really hurts my hands.

Let's look at these questions:

- Has Jimmy had a good day?
- Does he feel that he has achieved things today?
- Has the adult been aware of Jimmy's needs and consequently provided appropriate resources and challenges?
- Is Jimmy confident about himself as a capable little learner?
- Would Jimmy, given the choice, come back tomorrow? Would you?

And this is or could be happening to thousands of Jimmys every day – makes you think, doesn't it?

Addressing the issues

So how can we address these issues? A very simple task is the '**I am, I need**' evaluation. This needs to be carried out with the entire team and can be utilised for numerous purposes; here it is for looking at boys.

You will need a large piece of A1 paper and some markers. In the centre of the paper together draw a picture of a boy and all the aspects and characteristics of that child, how they are moving, what they might be wearing and carrying etc. The drawing is a bit of fun so do not get too carried away with detail. It might be a child that you know or an amalgamation of children in your setting.

I AM FOUR

loud

adventurous

affectionate

talkative

demanding

ego-centric

physical

good at guessing

demonstrative

busy

fun

imaginative

I NEED

space

time

open-ended resources

sensitive adults

hugs and reassurance

problems to solve

things to move about

Now the thinking comes into play – decide on an age for your child and start to list all the characteristics of that child on one edge of the paper. I would strongly recommend that you list the positives here – for as we know our starting points for learning and provision are what the children *can do*.

Having decided on these attributes and characteristics, start to list all the things the child will need in order for all these factors to be met.

The list is endless, but it will assist in breaking down all the individual aspects of the child.

The next part of the process is key for you. The next section focuses on you – having discussed all these issues, and worked out that the child is a combination of all these complex attributes you need to think about your role.

Now my role is to provide for them – how do you do this? This will take in-depth analysis of your school/setting, the resources, and the staff deployment, who works best with which children, the routines and the expectations – of both the children and the adults.

We know that boys are demanding of adult attention, that their emotions are expressed through action rather than talk, that they prefer to lie down to work and are more interested in objects and things than faces and emotions. They also prefer to build things high rather than out, they see into the distance rather than close up, they use less speech but have greater speech problems and they like to watch each other in order to imitate and innovate ideas.

Boys are a complex bunch, they do not fit into one category and we must be very much aware of stereotyping. We cannot think that '*Oh it's just what boys do, they all do that*'. They might or they might not. Each child is unique and must be approached with that in mind.

This chapter has scratched the surface of why boys do what they do, and think how they think. It must be remembered that not all boys are the same; there are differences between boys just as there are differences between the genders. What I hope to have discussed in this chapter is broad developmental and gender factors that practitioners must be aware of if they are to succeed in assisting our young males achieve the best they possibly can.

What is the nature of a boy?

2 : Why are boys underachieving?

In answering this question I think we have to address a number of issues: Why are boys underachieving? What do we mean by achievement? Are boys in fact underachieving, or are they merely operating at the levels they should be, given their relatively young age at the end of the Foundation Stage and Key Stage One? Is unhelpful comparison with girls actually benefitting anybody or simply putting more stress on boys and practitioners?

Boys' perceptions of themselves

Carol Dweck's (1999) assertion:

> 'The view you adopt of yourself profoundly affects the way you lead your life'

must be at the forefront of practitioners' minds when dealing with young boys. They need to be asking:

- What messages are we giving boys about their competence as learners?
- To what extend do we value their natural drive and physicality?
- Are we using interests as starting points for learning journeys?

If the answers to these three questions are resounding uncertainty then there are many issues that the setting will need to address in order to build up boys' self-confidence, self-esteem and self-perception of themselves as capable young people, with valid view-points, concerns and interests. Building confidence and self-esteem should be the main purpose of all early years provision. We should be looking to the future. What are we putting in place that will allow the children the opportunity to achieve well in the future, once they have left our settings and schools and moved into the big wide world?

Getting it right for boys

The DfES guidance *Promoting Children's Mental Health within Early Years and School Settings* (2001) defines children who are mentally healthy as those who:

- 'develop psychologically, emotionally, intellectually and spiritually
- initiate, develop and sustain mutually satisfying personal relationships
- use and enjoy solitude
- become aware of others and empathise with them
- play and learn
- develop a sense of right and wrong
- resolve (face) problems and setbacks and learn from them.'

I do think that this is a very useful document as it deals with the core issues at hand and the core principles that should be at the heart of educational practice. The duty of schools and practitioners is to ensure that children see themselves as capable, that they have resilience to combat set-backs, and strategies with which to overcome hurdles and challenges. It is not so much a matter of what you know but rather how you *use* what you know to your best advantage and continue to learn and discover as you go forward.

Differences between boys and girls

In 2009 the National Strategies published *Gender and Education – Myth Busters,* a decidedly unhelpful document that, when summarised, pointed to the conclusion that there is no discernable difference between the genders and it is a matter of effective pedagogy (unfortunately missing in many NVQ and ITT courses). What the document patently failed to do was to address the reasons why so many young males are underachieving. It alluded to socio-cultural factors and stereotyping, but did not explore the more ethereal concepts of self-belief, persistence, confidence and capability.

However, it must be noted that we live in a society where there remain stereotypical definitions of femininity and masculinity. Boys are 'meant' to be automatically tough and resilient, which makes it incredibly difficult for a young male to talk about feelings and emotions.

Too many boys, at very early ages, have unrealistic masculine concepts foisted upon them. They start to understand that to be emotional or uncertain equates to being 'a girl'. So they learn, from a very early age, to supress feelings and concerns which unequivocally leads to real issues and barriers being cemented in place. This stops them from fully developing a comprehensive range of emotional responses.

Despite best intentions and whatever we like to think to the contrary, we live in a society where the majority of practitioners treat boys and girls differently and adults do not view boys' play as learning, but rather something to be tolerated for short periods of time. Studies have shown that as babies, girls tend to get cuddled more than boys, and that boys invariably get smacked far more often, and harder, than girls.

Adults tend to discourage emotional awareness in boys, unintentional as it may be, but it remains a fact. The language that adults use with girls is far more emotionally charged, as adults we are far more attentive if a girl is upset or had a tumble. With boys it is more of a matter of 'Get on with it, stop crying and be a brave little chap'.

Respecting the differences

This chapter focuses on the need for stimulating adults who engage meaningfully with children – where speaking and listening underpins practice. We have to view boys' behaviour and strengths for what they are, not something to be discouraged for the sake of a quieter or more compliant classroom or play area. We have to accept difference. For it is only when differences are truly recognised, respected and catered for that patterns of similarity in provision and learning can be found.

Remember that at early ages children do choose gender-specific roles – they are learning to be themselves in a real-life social context. We know that to give boys and girls equal rights in the early years means to give them different and specific opportunities. It is not sufficient to say everything is open to all children, since at this age children choose gender-specific activities.

Think about the learning opportunities in the role play area and indeed what types of role play you have on offer for the children to use, practise things with and to get a bigger vision of themselves as learners. Many schools and settings will have a home corner (and I have nothing against a home corner) but what I do object to is the learning opportunities they offer all children, particularly boys, if there is not another opportunity for role play available.

The majority of the time it is the girls who will be in the home corner, and it is a fairly female-dominated area of play. Girls' greater language and emotional competency allows them to take control of this environment. Boys will play in the home corner but I urge you to look at the learning they are undertaking and the roles they are portraying.

Boys will often be organised by girls to take on less active and passive roles, '*I am mummy, she is daddy and you can be... the dog or the baby!*' Brilliant! We now have a pack of dogs roaming the setting woofing and barking! Or a plethora of babies wailing and screaming – joyous! The next thing the adult does is go around saying, '*No dogs thank you – find something else to do*'. Find something else! There is nothing else. So my whole morning might be spent as a dog – where is the learning? When the little fellow goes home and mum asks him what he did today, '*Well I was a dog. I barked and yelped all day*'. What fun!? He really did not achieve or learn very much today at all.

It is important to have various role plays around the setting, both indoors and out. Some of these will become gender specific, and this is fine, children are imitating what they see. They are learning about themselves as individuals and how they fit into the wider society. As an adult you will also be able to gauge real contextualised learning as skills and knowledge are honed and practised in meaningful application. There is more discussion about this in Chapter Four.

Steve Biddulph in *Raising Boys* (2010) makes an interesting observation that boys will often feel insecure and in danger if there is not enough structure in a situation. Left to their own devices they will start to jostle and play will fall away as they seek to establish a hierarchy. This could be construed as the natural order of things, however if learning is to be consolidated and integrated into the psyche, routines and good adult interactions are paramount.

During my time coaching boys at rugby I found this to be true, not only of the younger children but teenagers and adults alike. I had to ensure that sessions were meticulously planned, that one activity or practice drill seamlessly led to another, that all the drills and games were short in time and that they built up to a bigger picture. I could not start with the bigger picture but rather had to incrementally add bits to it so it became clear that step by step this was happening. If I was not on top of my game the sessions would quickly fall apart, the boys would be running about all over the place, jumping on top of each other, jostling and establishing hierarchies – it was amazing to watch.

A tale of a boy's learning and adult intervention

I did an observation of a reception class during the spring term. The children were all settled in and the school was particularly fortunate to have three adults supporting in the class.

The theme was traditional stories, good for language development and narrative and the particular story the children were learning about was Little Red Riding Hood. The classroom was well-resourced. The role play area was Grandma's house and there were small world play and table-top talking activities set up. The children also had opportunities to retell the story and make their own versions (key words were out in the environment).

As I sat there I noted that one practitioner was taking a focus group – the focus of which was to retell and sequence the story. I also noted that there were no boys inside the classroom. They were all outside playing... transformers.

I ventured outside to be greeted by the sight of two practitioners deep in conversation, while the boys were left to their own devices. Initially the play was of quite high order – lots of conversations and discussions about who was going to be who and what was going to unfold in the play. The adults meanwhile carried on their in-depth discussion.

As the play moved on and became more boisterous and loud the adults decided it was time to intervene. Intervention in terms of 'Stop running', 'Put that back' and 'No thank you', rather than in-depth interaction with the play to stimulate and take the learning forward. They were in short 'policing' the play with no real interest in how it progressed or regressed.

And regress it did because there was no added structure or meaningful interventions – jostling started and the play degenerated.

The boys were then called into the focus activity to retell the story of Little Red Riding Hood. Well, you can imagine the distinct lack of enthusiasm. One minute I am 'Optimus Prime the destroyer of worlds', the next I have to talk about grandma and a wolf? It's just confusing. No doubt a label was written that some of the boys, 'Found it difficult to concentrate and retell a story'.

The point I am making here illustrates a number of issues:

1. The boys' ideas were not being utilised as starting points for learning.
2. Adults were not conducive to the action-based play and did not tolerate it.
3. Adults did not mediate in the play, support or extend it.
4. These boys were retelling stories and concentrating – but it was not recognised.
5. Through lack of sensitive adult engagement the play degenerated.

What is achievement?

The key objectives have to be:

- educating the whole child and 'hopefully' sustaining a life-long interest in education rather than short-term gains of examination or summative assessment success.
- working with the most vulnerable boys in our education system, not just so that they can survive the system but in preparation for life beyond schooling.
- fostering and developing a positive disposition and attitude towards learning.

Learning in New Zealand

It is interesting to look at the *New Zealand Curriculum* (2007). It is a fascinating document which states the following:

'Our vision is for young people:

- who will be creative, energetic, and enterprising
- who will seize the opportunities offered by new knowledge and technologies to secure a sustainable social, cultural, economic, and environmental future for our country
- who will work to create an Aotearoa New Zealand in which Māori and Pākehā recognise each other as full Treaty partners, and in which all cultures are valued for the contributions they bring
- who, in their school years, will continue to develop the values, knowledge, and competencies that will enable them to live full and satisfying lives
- who will be confident, connected, actively involved, and lifelong learners.'

The document goes on to stress that children will be:

- 'positive in their own identity
- motivated and reliable
- resourceful
- enterprising and entrepreneurial
- resilient.'

The document uses a lovely phrase, 'connected', which in essence means:

- 'able to relate well to others
- effective users of communication tools
- connected to the land and environment
- members of communities
- international citizens.'

The document stresses that all children will be Lifelong learners, which includes being:

- 'literate and numerate
- critical and creative thinkers
- active seekers, users, and creators of knowledge.'

The National Curriculum of New Zealand identifies five key life-long competencies:

Getting it right for boys

- Thinking
- Using language, symbols, and texts
- Managing self
- Relating to others
- Participating and contributing and being informed decision makers

This is backed by an effective pedagogy that will:

- create a supportive learning environment
- encourage reflective thought and action
- enhance the relevance of new learning
- facilitate shared learning
- make connections to prior learning and experience
- provide sufficient opportunities to learn
- inquire into the teaching–learning relationship.

The underlying messages are about thinking *about* thinking and promoting positive dispositions in children. Learning for children is inseparable from its social and cultural context. Children learn best when they feel accepted, when they enjoy positive relationships with their peers and adults, when there is a 'can-do' culture in the setting or school, and when they are able to be active, visible members of the learning community.

Children learn most effectively when they develop the ability to stand back from the information or ideas that they have engaged with and think about these objectively. We need to ask, are we giving our boys the opportunity to reflect on their learning?

Reflective learners assimilate new learning, relate it to what they already know, adapt it for their own purposes, and translate thought into action. Over time, children will develop their creativity, their ability to think critically about information and ideas, and their metacognitive ability (that is, their ability to think about their own thinking).

Teachers and practitioners should actively encourage such thinking when they design environments, challenges and opportunities that require children to critically evaluate the material they use and consider the purposes for which it was originally created and how they might use it in a different context.

What should we expect of children?

In England girls are continuing to outperform boys in every aspect of the Early Years Foundation Stage Profile (2008). Even in Physical and Creative Development, areas where boys should feel competent and confident, girls are making greater progress. Why is this?

- Are the scale descriptors too general and narrow and consequently do they not take into consideration physiological and cognitive differences?
- Are practitioners aware of differences and differentiating planning and expectation?
- Are expectations unrealistic for boys and developmentally inappropriate?

What is perhaps more concerning is the draft of the revised Early Years Foundation Stage and the utilisation of *'Emerging, Expected and Exceeding'* as descriptors for achievement. All children are *'emerging'* into something, in fact all adults are *emerging*, we should never stop *emerging*, but that does not make us work at the *expected* level. Life is about emerging and assimilating and learning new strategies and gaining new insights. When, if ever, do we *exceed*? Do we ever say, *'I better calm down now as I am exceeding myself!'* No we don't. You cannot judge a child to be exceeding expectations, that child is doing what they are doing at the level that suits them, our role is to ensure they have resources and support to continue or accelerate progress.

Exceeding expectation is like when you are going to a party, but do not really fancy it so your expectations are low – but lo and behold you have a great time. We cannot look at children in this way. Exceeding is done through comparison and if we continue to compare children rather than look at them as individuals our educational troubles will continue.

What do we expect of children? Do we want them to be exceeding all the time? Do we want a four-year-old to be operating at the level of a six-year-old, and a ten-year-old operating like a thirteen-year-old? As an adult I do not think, *'Good grief, I am 45, but developmentally I am only 30 – better get a move on'*. It is worrying that without very skilful practitioners some children will be assessed as constantly underachieving and be on a treadmill of failure.

Getting it right for boys

The education establishment has to respond and help boys to realise their true potential by offering a meaningful experiential curriculum that caters for the more physical and hands-on nature of young boys' learning, that takes account of cognitive and physical differences and allows equal access to it. Otherwise we run the very real risk of producing future generations of disaffected boys who are unable to assimilate new skills and knowledge, to empathise, to see themselves as capable and creative or to think imaginatively.

The historical background

As a society we have swung like a pendulum from one extreme to the other in our educational thinking. During the 1970s and 1980s most of the focuses of gender were orientated towards girls' participation in education and careers as they were often under-represented in both areas. The achievements of girls should be celebrated, as many interventionist programmes that were created to address the issues were considered enormously successful. In fact, some would argue that as a direct result of these programmes boys may have suffered.

It is only in the last six to eight years that boys have become the focus of research and education intervention as attention has shifted to their learning and the existence of a gender gap. Girls, on average, are currently achieving far higher levels of success in virtually all levels of education and subjects than boys. This has had the unfortunate consequence of simplistically comparing boys with girls, resulting in the inappropriate labelling of boys as 'underachievers'.

How boys learn

If we think about how boys work and learn, on the whole, course work has been a disaster for them as long-term planning and time management are not great strengths. Invariably there is a last-minute panic and rush. As previously noted, boys are less receptive than girls to oral feedback or over-complicated instruction – too much information can lead to confusion, instability and emotional turmoil.

Think about feedback to children, this is especially true of older boys – how much information is given? There might be four or five areas to improve on. However, by the time the adult gets to the third point (verbally or written) the young chap has switched off already. Consequently any resubmitted work would only deal with the first two points for 'improvement', not all of it. The result – well they would have to do it again, and slowly that child would start to give up as they *can never get it right*.

The Early Years Foundation Stage Profile (2008) highlights two crucial statements under the Dispositions and Attitudes section of the Personal, Social and Emotional Development strand:

- children being able to maintain concentration for prolonged periods of time *and*
- continuing to be motivated and interested in learning.

It is a child's undeniable right to be afforded the possibility of achieving these two statements in order for them to become successful life-long learners, yet the percentage of boys who do not achieve these two points is alarming. Again the question has to be *why*? Statistics from the Early Years Profile would have us believe that a sizeable percentage of five-year-old boys cannot maintain concentration and are not interested, excited and motivated about learning. Anecdotal and observational evidence would say differently. One just has to observe boys who are meaningfully engaged in an activity.

A little case study – learning based on fascination

This is Patrick, he is three. Patrick had been driving his bike around the garden and decided to make a map of where he had been. He found the large card and the pens from the writing area and started to draw.

I could hear him muttering under his breath, 'Under, over... around the tree'. He drew the shape of his ride around the garden and added further shapes and marks as he talked to himself. He took his map and tried it out, running round the garden following its instructions. Jacob followed him on the bike, fascinated by what Patrick was doing. Patrick came to the end of his map: 'I need more...', he mused and went back to add more.

Jacob joined him and they shared the map-making with each other.

Getting it right for boys

What learning was happening here? Why could it happen?

- **Motivated and interested** – most definitely.
- **Maintaining concentration** – yes indeed.
- **Emotional well-being, being sure of what he was doing** – yes, lots of this.
- **Mathematical positional language** – by the bucket load.
- **Use of language to modify thinking and problem solve** – most certainly.
- **Physical development in bike riding and emergent mark-making** – one should think so.
- **Social development, allowing his peer to join in the play** – great evidence of this.

The reason Patrick was so at ease with his mission and his learning was that he was emotionally secure in the setting, the resources and challenges were appropriate and pitched at the right level, he had time to practise, and there were sensitive adults who had noted his interests and provided accordingly.

It really is a matter of practitioners re-evaluating what the learning looks like and having empathy and understanding with the more physical and boisterous nature of boys' learning. Patrick was displaying great inner confidence, expressing his thoughts and ideas in a physical way – he walked around with his map – he is three and already picking up evidence towards the Foundation Stage Profile.

Some theories

There are many theories for why boys are underachieving:

- Poor boys – this theory proposes that some boys are victims of a changing society.
- Failing schools, failing boys – there appears to be a link between poorly performing schools and poor performance by some boys.
- Boys will be boys – boys are part of a changing society with a redefining of the role of males being central to this. As such, boys should be allowed to change and evolve at their own pace.

Two main theories are central to the discussion of supporting boys in their learning. The first is that boys have failed to change with society whereas girls have become empowered and are the new optimistic generation while boys have remained in a previous culture, which is at odds with our society today. The second theory is that boys have rejected existing cultures and have formed a sub-culture based on 'laddism'.

The truth is that the topic is more complex than believing that boys belong to one or other cultures. What is clear is that there is a lot of misinformation generally perpetuated by the media about boys and, if anything, they as a group still have many of the same aspirations and interests they have always had. The difference is that society has changed and many of their aspirations are at odds with current trends. What appears to be happening with certain groups of boys is that they are remaining rooted in a previous culture that may no longer be appropriate or they are forming new sub-cultures as in 'laddism'. This theory suggests that boys will be boys and we should not expect anything else.

Some boys achieve highly, some girls achieve poorly – but the underlying trend is that of male underachievement. Emotional stability and regulation are central to achievement – to achieve, a person must have a positive self-image and strong internal motivation. There is a propensity to discourage emotional development within boys – statements such as 'brave lad, mummy's little soldier, who's a big boy then?' run counter to the males' need for reaffirmation and reassurance.

The primary and early years workforce is dominated by women. There are a sizeable percentage of young male learners who will not come across a positive male role model until they reach junior school or later into secondary school. Given this fact, it is not difficult to see why there are so many boys underachieving – they are not receiving a balanced outlook and genuine understanding. In extreme cases they learn that from an early age what they do naturally is usually deemed inappropriate.

Continuing problems

When considering the learning needs of boys, it is worth remembering that while the Early Years Foundation Stage Profile (2008) results point to progress over time by both genders, the gap between the two continues to be ever-increasing despite numerous books, articles, research, debate and shop-floor training for practitioners. Something is not right, and boys continue to be labelled as underachieving.

Other research, however, has gone further and reached much bleaker conclusions.

According to the I CAN review *The Cost to the Nation of Children's Poor Communication* (2006) children are entering nursery and reception classes at lower physical and cognitive levels than they were even five years ago, and more than half have impoverished language. It is vital to remember that boys from birth have a smaller vocabulary and a lower threshold for listening. This lack of communication skills in boys is very pronounced.

Work by Gary Wilson, *Raising Boys' Achievement* (2007) has identified various barriers to boys' learning, including a lack of independence and, significantly, a lack of emotional development stemming from poorer language skills. Girls use between 10 and 30 times more expressive language in their play. *What are you doing about this* and how are you supporting boys' language and emotional development? This is the focus of the next chapter.

Brain development

Let's carry on with the discussion on brain development from the previous chapter and how the brain of a boy is wired differently from a girl. This could be one of the myriad reasons why boys are 'under-achieving'.

Here are some fascinating facts to aid your practice and understanding of the complex issues surrounding boys' learning:

- For girls, the *corpus callosum* (the connecting bundle of tissues between hemispheres) is, on average, larger than a boy's – up to 25 per cent larger by adolescence. This enables more 'cross talk' between hemispheres in the female brain.
- Girls have, in general, stronger neural connectors in their temporal lobes than boys have. These connectors lead to more sensually

detailed memory storage, better listening skills, and better discrimination among the various tones of voice. This leads, among other things, to greater use of detail in writing assignments.

- The *hippocampus* (another memory storage area in the brain) is larger in girls than in boys, increasing girls' learning advantage, especially in the language arts.
- Girls' prefrontal cortex is generally more active than boys' and develops at an earlier age. For this reason, girls tend to make fewer impulsive decisions than boys do. Further, girls have more serotonin in the bloodstream and the brain, which makes them biochemically less impulsive.
- Girls generally use more cortical areas of their brains for verbal and emotive functioning. Boys tend to use more cortical areas of the brain for spatial and mechanical functioning (Moir and Jessel, 1989; Rich, 2000).

Because boys' brains have more cortical areas dedicated to spatial-mechanical functioning, males use, on average, half the brain space that females use for verbal-emotive functioning. Does this sound familiar? The cortical trend toward spatial-mechanical functioning makes many boys want to move objects through space, like balls, model airplanes, or just their arms and legs. Most boys, although not all of them, will experience words and feelings differently than girls do (Blum, 1997; Moir and Jessel, 1989).

Boys lateralise brain activity. Their brains not only operate with less blood flow than girls' brains, but they are also structured to compartmentalise learning. So, girls tend to multitask better than boys, with fewer attention span problems and greater ability to make quick transitions between lessons (Havers, 1995).

The male brain is set to renew, recharge, and reorient itself by entering what neurologists call a rest state. The boy in the back of the classroom whose eyes are drifting toward sleep has entered a neural rest state. It is predominantly boys who drift off without completing assignments, who stop taking notes and fall asleep during a lecture, or who tap pencils or otherwise fidget in the hope of keeping themselves awake and learning.

Getting it right for boys

Females tend to recharge and reorient neural focus without rest states. So, a girl can be bored with a lesson, but she will nonetheless keep her eyes open, take notes, and perform relatively well. This is especially true when the adult uses more words to teach a lesson instead of being spatial and diagrammatic. The more words an adult uses, the more likely boys are to 'zone out' or go into rest state. The male brain is better suited for symbols, abstractions, diagrams, pictures, and objects moving through space than for the monotony of words (Gurian, 2001).

This last issue is incredibly important for practitioners. As the early years workforce is predominantly female, the methodology of learning and teaching will automatically follow the pattern of what females know best, how they do things and what works well for them. If practitioners are not self-reflective and analytical about their learning and teaching methodologies, then the same practice will be repeated time and time again with boys in particular being asked to conform and adhere to behaviour and thinking patterns that cut against the grain of what it is to be a young male learner.

I would hope that you are starting to reflect on how you work with the multitude of children in your settings and schools. What does real differentiation look like? Are you allowing certain modes of play to happen that might very well challenge your assumptions and beliefs of what good learning looks like?

Further issues to address

There are some further issues that need to be addressed if we are to unpick this question of boys underachieving:

- Parker, in 1995, prior to the onset of the Early Years Foundation Stage and back in the realms of 'Desirable Outcomes' (remember them and the thin blue document? I have been into settings where this is still used) stated that there was real concern among early years experts that the National Curriculum and testing could breed a generation of super girly girls and disaffected boys. He feared that school would end up suiting girls more than boys due to the learning and teaching pedagogy – I think that Parker's concerns have indeed come to fruition.

- Physiological differences between boys and girls are not being taken into account. The testosterone rushes of four and fourteen are being marginalised and boys' desire for physicality is not being addressed by practitioners who are reluctant to participate in play that they are not 100 per cent happy with.

- Recent research shows that on average in early years settings girls are 'praised' 70 per cent more often than boys. Boys will also be 'chastised' up to 70 per cent more often than girls in terms of '*Stop that, put it back, keep quiet*' – all adding to the depressing scenario that 'I am, as a boy, not very good at doing stuff'.

- Add to this nice little mix the undeniable fact that boys are too often stereotyped through appearance. It would be well worth your while to note this. In the previous chapter we met Jimmy and went through Jimmy's day, now add on to this that his endeavours and hard work are far less likely to be recognised and praised by adults from whom he craves affection. A very useful task to do with your setting is for a system of adult observations to be done on all staff members on how they talk to and positively enhance children's self-esteem – who do they spend more time talking to and what is the nature and content of those conversations?

- Walkerdine (1983) argues that the reason girls show early success at school is that they take up the right positions in the pedagogic discourse, while boys do not. Boys stay silent and do not take part in the domestic games which are being taught by those who are used to a domestic play setting. She also suggests that boys clearly do not feel at home in domestic imaginative situations, as girls have the controlling hand. She found that boys often wanted to remove themselves from domestic play or change the play because they were subservient.

- Millard (1997) argues that reading is seen as an activity more appropriate to girls than boys and that boys and girls create different educational experiences for themselves. Boys create more discipline problems for teachers, primarily due to inadequate provision, and consequently take up more of the teachers' time, therefore actively opposing teachers giving girls equal time.

- Paley (1988) came to the conclusion that the curriculum she offered suited girls more than boys. Girls would go to tables associated with 'work', while boys would avoid such activities. For girls the work at the table is play, and they will use the equipment whether the teacher is there or not.

- O'Sullivan (1997) suggests that starting school earlier is bad news for boys who are not ready for more formal teaching, and that boys are more likely to be treated as part of a group rather than individually like girls.
- Boys' need for superhero play is not being met at school but, as Jordan (1995) describes, is perfectly normal behaviour for them. Through such games boys are discovering what being a boy and a man is all about.

Some possible solutions

- Offer themes and topics such as adventure, humour and sport in boys' reading and play matter. It is vital that you start from what they know and what they are doing. Embrace popular culture, it surrounds them, they live it and see it everywhere.
- Audit what books and reading materials you offer – who reads what, who is in the reading area more often?
- Adapt to the needs of boys, as boys are not ready to be sedentary in their learning at the same time as girls. Re-assess your routines and keep in mind the age plus two rule (see page 38), and question who are the routines there for, the adults or the children?
- Become more 'boy friendly', with regard to reading and mark making. Make reading more appealing to boys.
- Some 'underperforming' boys would do much better if they were given a richer, kinaesthetic learning diet from the beginning of their school life.
- The outdoor environment should play a central role in educating boys.
- Be aware of difference yourselves, approve of the different learning styles and embrace new ways to deliver the curriculum.
- Motivate boys to write by assisting in generating the need to write.

3 : The role of the adult

'The key is curiosity, and it is curiosity, not answers that we model. As we seek to know more about a child, we demonstrate the acts of observing, listening, questioning and wondering. When we are curious about a child's words and our responses to those words, the child feels respected. The child is respected. "What are the ideas that I have that are so interesting to the teacher? I must be somebody with good ideas".'

Vivian Paley (2007)

It is well worth asking this question: When was the last time you played? By that I mean when did you *really* play and lose yourself in another world? When did you became 'another', see things differently, lose track of time and become totally engaged and engrossed in what you were doing?

As adults we do not play enough. We are too concerned with the supposed realities and complexities of everyday life, of getting things done, of being busy, of being grown up. We lose the skills of 'transference' and pretence. We become inhibited, serious and responsible, with little time for creating different worlds or for being other people. Well, it's about time that we stopped *playing serious* and started to *seriously play* if we are going to inspire and model good practice for our boys!

Routines and expectations

I stated in the Introduction that it is my firm belief that it is not boys who are underachieving or failing, it is the adults and the environments, routines and unrealistic expectations that are failing the boys. I make no apology for this at all. Only too often have I visited schools and settings where the routines and expectations mitigate disastrously against boys'

learning – with long-term damaging effects on attainment, achievement and the desire to learn. Why is it that over 7000 more boys than girls each year leave school with no qualifications? Sadly this is a number that is constantly rising. More frighteningly 83 per cent of all school exclusions are boys – why?

In one of the schools I taught in years ago (a school with a very high level of deprivation and impoverished language and emotional development), there was a real issue with boys' attainment and achievement. At the time I was a Foundation Stage Coordinator and, as a team, we worked tirelessly with families to support boys' learning and to ensure that the boys saw themselves as capable learners. From extremely low starting points we ensured that children made outstanding progress and were capable of hitting Year One with the capacity and inclination to carry on the learning journey.

However, this onward journey never happened – the routines and expectations in Year One resulted in these boys sitting for prolonged periods of time, becoming 'fidgety' and 'disruptive' because the curriculum on offer was, to be frank, boring. I would then see these boys being kept in during playtime to complete the work, and then again at lunch time. What was the thinking?

What these boys needed more than anything else was space, physical movement and time, not more of the same. Our early work on self-esteem was rapidly undone. It was awful to watch. It was only following a revision of learning and teaching and effective pedagogy that this practice was changed so that the new classes met the needs of the children. The result was higher attainment for boys, greater engagement in the learning process and greater self-esteem.

The role of the adult is the vital ingredient in children's learning. You have the capacity and power to take a child's learning forward in leaps and bounds, to give them self-confidence and belief in their abilities. You also have the power and capacity to desensitise children's emotions. Your role is unbelievable, it is complex, it is emotional, it is demanding and, when done well, it is the most rewarding thing in the world.

How can you not want to play with a bunch of young mud-eating monsters, who want to explore, discover, be energetic, be loud and have fun? The fun definitely needs to go back into our interactions with boys.

It is not about policing their play, it is about purposefully interacting and engaging with it, with a view to extending it.

We want our young boys to grow up with a positive sense of identity and a positive disposition towards learning. They should have a 'can-do' attitude, because as young children they were surrounded by engaging, stimulating and sensitive adults who supported rather than negated their natural inherent drives of exploration, doing and being.

Reflecting on practice

You have to ask yourself and your team serious questions about whether you can actually redesign your philosophy to become part of the process of learning rather than a barrier to it:

- Are practitioners aware of the choices boys and girls make – what are these choices and how are they reflected equally in the learning environment?
- Observe the use of the physical environment and take action on your findings. Where does the learning happen, what sort of learning is taking place – how can I build on it? You will need to audit this so it will impact on your positive provision.
- Are there positive images around the environment that do not stereotype? (Although young children will play in gender specific roles at times.)

- Are there regular discussions with all parties to ensure inclusive practice?
- Are boys' and girls' choices valued equally – so that boys' interests are recognised, respected and validated as starting points for learning? This is extremely important, it is too easy to shy away from the large and boisterous and plump for something less challenging. Even if you have not yet learnt to love Batman or Transformers, you can learn some interesting things from watching them in play. Boys bring their own agendas; they get into some very active, very physically-involved games. They will imitate stories and popular culture and move on to innovating their own stories and adventures. Boys like to be people in authority, policemen, fire-fighters or super-heroes – embrace it!

Charlie and Spiderman story

Charlie was five. His mummy and daddy couldn't get a babysitter so they had to bring Charlie to a grown-ups' party. Charlie, being Charlie, got very bored after a short time – 'Can we go home now?' he kept requesting. Sometimes the grown-ups would talk to him and pick him up to play with him, but they were mostly busy talking and laughing with their friends.

There were no other kids there so Charlie was all alone in a room full of big people and he was getting restless. Suddenly daddy came over and said to Charlie, 'Why don't you wear your Spiderman suit, I'll help you get it from the car'.

Charlie loved Spiderman, he had all the comics and books, he'd seen the film and watched the cartoons. Charlie had spent the previous day making a Spiderman costume from all sorts of materials. He especially liked his 'Spideymask'. He had spent a long time cutting it out, measuring his head and colouring it in.

Charlie got his Spiderman costume from the car with his daddy and went off to put it on. Charlie was Spiderman – he was not Charlie anymore. He was 'Spidey' on important missions to save the world!

The grown-ups didn't see Charlie again all afternoon, well they saw Charlie, but Charlie was Spiderman – hiding under tables, lurking behind doors, talking to himself retelling stories, being in another place, in a wonderful imaginative world working at the very edge of his competencies – he was 'in the zone'. He was safe, secure, his needs were met and he could be in this 'other place'.

Charlie's daddy is a very good friend of mine and we were watching Spidey navigate the room and problem-solve his many imaginary issues. Daddy turned to me and pointed at Charlie saying, 'You see that there, that's living the dream'.

It was a turn of phrase that has had a profound impact on me ever since. Charlie *was* living the dream and it is our responsibility and duty of care to ensure that children when they are with us have the opportunity to live their dream. It is the entitlement of childhood.

It is well worth remembering Vygotsky's philosophy at this point:

- Learning is a social process – so how you model and transfer skills, knowledge and attitudes is crucial.
- Children learn through and with 'significant others', – for many children you will be that significant other, for they can be with you or in your setting for extremely long periods of time.
- Parents and families are important – how are you engaging with the families of boys and supporting them in understanding how their children are learning? This is crucial as many parents really need assistance in understanding why their two-year-old son is acting and behaving the way he does.
- *'Children at play are a head taller than themselves'* (Vygotsky, 1967) – what opportunities are you providing for children to be this 'head taller'? Are you supporting the development or hindering it?

Learning audit

I would strongly suggest that you do a learning audit in your setting, look in depth at the types of learning, the styles of learning and the areas of learning that the boys are engaging in or displaying. A simple format will suffice, nothing too complicated or time consuming, but something that will feed into meaningful action on behalf of the adults in the setting to support and co-construct the learning with the boys.

Getting it right for boys

LEARNING AUDIT			
Who was learning?	Where was the learning happening?	What was the learning?	Actions on observations
Bradley, George, Jim, Mohammed	In the construction area outside	Good interactions using talk to solve how they were going to build the brick wall. Problem solving, finding the right-sized bricks.	Provision for tomorrow – sand, plans, diagrams of buildings, pencils, clip boards. What will be my role in extending the play?

In the zone with Csikszentmihalyi

One of my favourite educational philosophers is Mihaly Csikszentmihalyi. His work centres on leisure sciences and his writings on enjoyment, *Beyond Boredom and Anxiety* (2000) have been translated into 20 different languages. One of his most recent works, *Flow in Sports* (1999), is the blueprint for professional coaches all over the world. Csikszentmihalyi's relevance to this book and to your thinking in settings and schools is his theory of the *State of Flow* which was the culmination of 40 years of research into the differing strains of 'fun' and what links all the aspects of fun together.

Csikszentmihalyi's *State of Flow* is linked to practitioner skill in matching skills, knowledge and competencies all together. It enables children to live the dream alluded to earlier and can be represented by a simple graph.

What the graph represents is the correlation between competency and challenge. If the child is very competent and the challenge is low then the child will be bored and depressed. Conversely if the challenge

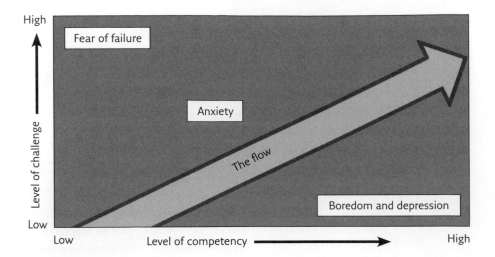

is high and the competency or development is low then the child will experience anxiety and fear of failure.

Think how this model affects the boys in your setting – do you have a framework for observations that looks at competencies and development issues and then do you have an environment in place as a result that meets the needs of those boys? When challenge meets competency 'deep level' learning takes place, where, according to Laevers the 'involved child is gaining a deep motivated, intense and long-term learning experience'.

We are in the flow!

It is when challenges are high and personal skills used to the utmost that this rare state of consciousness is achieved. The first symptom of flow is a narrowing of attention on a clearly-defined goal. We feel involved, concentrated, absorbed. We know what must be done and we get immediate feedback as to how well we are doing. Even a usually mundane and boring task can become exciting and involving once the challenges are brought into balance with the individual's skill and the goals are clarified.

The depth of concentration required by the fine balance of challenges and skills precludes worrying about temporarily irrelevant issues. The well-matched use of skills provides a sense of control over our actions; we often feel a sense of transcendence, as if the boundaries of the self have been expanded. In these moments the awareness of time disappears – this is flow and we are truly involved.

The majority of behaviour issues in early years settings are due to practitioners not matching competency with challenge – expectation is either too low or too high. How will a boy react to this, bearing in mind what we already know about the nature of a boy? That is:

- lack of language skills
- less emotional development and regulation
- physically 'unjoined' up and emotions expressed through action.

Observations

The adult's role is to guarantee that there is in place a rigorous system of observations. Children and boys in particular need to be observed regularly at self-initiated or adult-directed meaningful playful learning experiences. The vast majority of evidence towards progress and assessment will come from these observations. It is important that all children are observed as too often there are big gaps in children's records because observations have not been carried out. Practitioners will often have evidence for the more gregarious children or those that there are concerns about. However, it is the children that just 'get on' that are often missed out.

Routines must facilitate opportunities for observations. In pre-school about 75 per cent of a child's time should be spend on self-initiated learning. This is an awfully long time for adults to meaningfully engage with children and support, mediate and scaffold learning. *Does this happen in your setting?* Or are the routines hindering this expectation?

Good settings regularly observe children as a matter of course and these observations are then analysed, diagnosed and utilised to plan meaningful interventions or learning opportunities for the children – not next week or next month but rather tomorrow.

I would strongly recommend that you have a rolling system of observations. If you do not, too often children will get inadvertently 'missed'. You will have a ream of observations on children you have concerns about or on the most vocal members of the group but there is a big percentage of children that fall between these two categories – I call them the *'alright children'* because when you look at them they are alright, being busy and getting on with the process of learning. However, if we do not observe them or discuss them how can we take the learning and development forward and provide suitable challenges?

With this system all adults are aware of the children who are being observed, either as a focus, participant or for longer observations.

The cycle of learning and the role of the adult

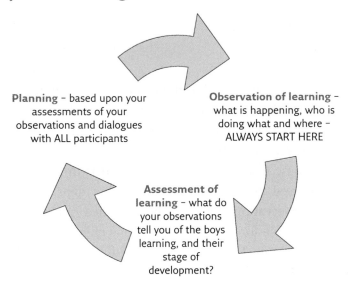

Planning – based upon your assessments of your observations and dialogues with ALL participants

Observation of learning – what is happening, who is doing what and where – ALWAYS START HERE

Assessment of learning – what do your observations tell you of the boys learning, and their stage of development?

Getting it right for boys

The rolling rota of observation

Week 1

Monday	Tuesday	Wednesday	Thursday	Friday
John	Mohammed	Porsche	Indira	Bert
Ismael	Shaheen	Mercedes	Harry	Ernie
Billy	April	Mondeo	Alfie	Kermit
Sarah	Michael	Jack	Mandy	Sharon
Chantelle	Linda	Patricia	Sophie	June

Week 2

Monday	Tuesday	Wednesday	Thursday	Friday
Bert	John	Mohammed	Porsche	Indira
Ernie	Ismael	Shaheen	Mercedes	Harry
Kermit	Billy	April	Mondeo	Alfie
Sharon	Sarah	Michael	Jack	Mandy
June	Chantelle	Linda	Patricia	Sophie

The rest of the children are *not* being ignored but will rather have significant 'catch as you can' achievement observations.

At the end of the session you may well have three to four observations per child. The key is to have a system whereby the observations are put straight into the child's record so they can be acted upon immediately.

In too many of the schools and settings I visit, I see plastic wallets or folders or the proverbial 'observation box' all stuffed full with observations of children. What are they doing in there – are they assisting the planning and provision, are they impacting on the practice? They can't be. These observations will be taken home at the weekend, when adults are trying to watch *Strictly Come Dancing* or the *X Factor* and will be stuck in children's records.

The point of the observation has been missed. The message has to be: *I've seen this today, how can I build upon or extend it tomorrow?* That is outstanding practice. Planning as a result is fluid and directed by children's interactions with the learning.

A point to note – *planning is about the learning, not the activity*. What are the learning opportunities I am looking to facilitate and develop by having these activities out? Think of *Stickle Bricks*. Boys play with this when they are two, when they are three, and when they are four and five – what is the difference in expectations? Same resource but a different expectation – please be aware of this and do not have a list of 'table fillers' that are trotted out every day.

Think *what* are the learning opportunities I am affording the children and *why* are they doing the task.

Empathy

To be an outstanding practitioner you will require EMPATHY. This involves being sensitive, moment by moment, to the changing needs and meaning which flow in another person; to the fear or rage or tenderness they might be experiencing. You will need to have confidence in your own ability and in yourself as a confident companion to the person... you lay aside yourself.

The key thing about empathy, true empathy, is that it is a complex, demanding and strong, yet also a subtle and gentle way of being. It is not condoning or condemning; it is challenging the other person. In order to be truly empathetic to the needs of young boy learners we need to have high levels of emotional maturity. It is well worth asking the staff in your setting: *How well do you know yourself?*

We each have an immediate likely response to a problem situation, which is likely to fit one of the following descriptions.

I'm stupid!!	I can't do this!!
Get an expert	Make a plan
I can fix it!	It's nothing to do with me!
What has worked before?	If only you hadn't...
Why oh why does it always happen to me?!	

Each of these initial responses leads us to respond in a particular way to the problem. While we may not be able to change our first feeling, we can acknowledge that by sticking to that response, we are limiting the possible options we have for sorting the problem out.

One of the most difficult problems we have to work with is likely to be resolving conflict concerning both adults and children. Our initial feelings about conflict will also influence how we respond to the situation.

There are a variety of feelings raised by seeing or being involved in conflict:

- anxiety
- fear
- excitement
- anger
- determination.

Like problem solving, we also have a pattern of response to conflict which may fit one of the following descriptions:

- run away
- give as good as you get
- ask someone for help
- refuse to get involved
- pretend it's not happening
- talk through the problem, listen to the other view and negotiate a resolution.

A child's perspective

Your role is to make your learning environment and the learning experiences as stimulating and as fun as you possibly can. To ensure you do this you need to look at things from a child's perspective:

- Physical organisation of the room – consider height and think about visual images and displays.
- Set up activities which involve the children describing the setting.
- Review the routines of the day and find out what the children's expectations are within these routines

- Make a collection of frequently-used phrases and consider the impact they have on children – both generally and individually.
- Identify acceptable ways available to children in the setting to say they do not want to take part in an activity, do not want to play with another child, to say they feel cross, angry and so on.
- Identify an approach and a consistent process to use in response to conflict situations. Check for learning opportunities for the children in the process.
- Use key phrases and adult role-modelling as a basis for initial social learning activities.
- Find ways to ask for and listen to children's views.

Active learning and 'possibility thinking'

There are a couple of statements in the Early Years Profile (2008) which can be found under the Problem Solving, Reasoning and Numeracy heading – the statement cuts across all three strands of this area and reads:

> *'Uses developing mathematical ideas and methods to solve practical problems'.*

It is a fantastic statement and should underpin all Foundation Stage practice, in fact if you remove the term 'mathematical' it reads even better:

> *Uses developing ideas and methods to solve practical problems.*

This is the very essence of our role as early years practitioners: to free children up and to enable them to become problem solvers and active learners with the ability to think about thinking.

The nurturing of children's creativity involves the close scrutiny of the processes of meaning and knowledge construction for each learner. Adults need to recognise the sheer creative engagement manifested by young learners, as they move beyond the given, or *'what is'*, to the possible, or to *'what could be'*. It is a matter of having *possibility as the core of creativity* central to your setting's values.

Encouraging boys to think for themselves

There are many ways to go about solving problems. Encouraging children to come up with alternative ways of approaching a problem uses intelligence and promotes creativity. It also facilitates the reflective aspect of autonomous action. As children generate different solutions to problems, they determine which is the best method and why. This process of evaluating possible solutions leads children to reconstruct their understanding of the situation – which promotes learning.

I witnessed an example of this in a reception class. A group of boys were fascinated with minibeasts and grubs. They had been looking at pictures of them in the non-fiction books and were intent on trying to find them. The teacher in the room was a very skilful practitioner who understood the needs of the boys and was willing to involve them in the planning.

This was a very simple process and used a very simple format. She had a discussion with the boys about what they knew about the bugs and listed the information. She then asked the boys what they would like to find out.

WHAT WE KNOW	WHAT WE WANT TO KNOW
Bugs fly.	Are bees and wasps the same?
They eat worms.	Can they fly backwards?
They have millions of legs.	Do they sleep?
Some are called millipedes.	What is the biggest bug?
They have different colours.	Do people eat them?
Some live in the ground.	
They have eggs.	

As an example of the high-level thinking, one child asked: *'What about Spiderman? Is he a bug? Cos he is then he ain't'* A genius question if ever there was one, and one that allowed the child to explore Spiderman and simultaneously condoned superhero play.

The best part of the process was left to last: *How will we know what we know and how to record it?*

It was jointly decided to design and make the 'ultimate bug' – so success criteria followed, success criteria decided by the boys.

WHAT MAKES A GOOD BUG?

Big wings	Different colours
Lots of legs	Feelers on the head
A big mouth for eating	And so on...
Lots of teeth	

The planning in effect had been done, the children had decided, with sensitive adult input on the success criteria, and off they went to research, design and construct their own ultimate bugs.

This principle of *What makes good...* should be utilised throughout your setting as it allows children to self-assess against shared criteria that they have had a part in developing.

It can cover many things:

What makes a good... sentence?
What makes a good... friend?
What makes a good... story?
What makes a good... listener?

The list is endless and the principle acts as an excellent way of helping the children to see themselves as learners. This is true autonomy.

What is autonomy?

Kamii (1984) says that *'autonomy is being governed by oneself'*. It is acting in accordance with oneself, in a freely-chosen, self-regulated way and accepting full responsibility for one's actions. It is the motivation behind the action, not the action itself that determines autonomy. The goal is for children to act with personal conviction about what is right. Autonomy means that children determine the right thing to do based on beliefs and understanding.

The autonomous thinking in the 'bug' example is encouraged by children exchanging points of view, and therefore looking at things from a variety of perspectives. The process involved in simultaneously considering the merits of differing viewpoints is at the heart of autonomous decision making. It was facilitated by the mutuality and reciprocity in relationships, in which individuals felt free to express ideas knowing that personal relationships were not at stake, and that all viewpoints were worth consideration, though some might need refining.

Helping children to forge friendships supports the skills of cooperation and negotiation that promotes autonomy. Children consequently learn to use democratic practices to solve problems rather than relying on the adult as the authority. Many practitioners see this as reducing the adult power in the setting. It often cuts across deeply-held beliefs on what their role is as a practitioner and early educator. The point has to be made that children do not know what they do not know, and do not learn by osmosis. *Developing autonomy and thinking about thinking is the key role for all practitioners.*

Theoretically it echoes Vygotsky's (1967),work and stresses the social context of learning, the importance of assessing the effectiveness of the adult as a critical participant in children's learning in order to enhance the cognitive level of this learning. Vygotskian theory holds that just as we use physical tools such as hammers and spanners to gain mastery over the physical world, we also use mental tools to extend our ability to think and communicate. It is the teaching of learning, not just the teaching of knowledge.

Leonid Venger (1967), a disciple of Vygotsky stated that getting ready for school is not about being able to read, write and count, but rather being able to learn *how* to read, write and count.

The zone of proximal development (ZPD)

This is the crux of Vygotsky's work, and is so crucial to any discussion on the role of the adult in children's learning. In scientific terms, it relates to the distance between the actual developmental level as determined by independent problem solving and the level of potential as determined through problem solving with adult guidance (or in collaboration with more able peers). All sounds a bit Latin?

But it's not really. It feeds into your role as a mediator in children's learning, the support and scaffolding you offer them, to your sensitivity, your empathy and your engagement in the learning process. During an observation or dialogue/interaction with children you might note what they are doing and how – your role then would be to sensitively add extra skills and competencies to any given situation. I have said it before but children do not know what they do not know and skilful adults support the development of independence and autonomy by offering sensitive co-operative interactions.

The strength of the ZPD is that it characterises mental and physical development prospectively, not retrospectively. Education in this country is based upon retrospection. SATs, GCSEs and so on judge you on what you know at a particular time, which pays no attention to future development or possibilities. Is it any wonder that we have disaffected teenager boys? The ZPD defines those functions that are in the process of maturing.

Getting it right for boys

Within the ZPD the child is working at their optimum level. With adult or peer assistance the child makes that next step in learning. Adult engagement is a vital component in Vygotskian theory. To Vygotsky, language is vital in mental development. Vygotsky argued that language liberated humans from the immediate experiences and built upon previous experiences and cultural history.

He pointed to a development of language and thinking skills, where the language leads to thinking:

- Private speech – children verbalise their play and thought as they internalise information and integrate new ideas
- Internal speech – when the thought process is 'in the head'
- Verbal thought – the shortening of words for symbols.

Many adults, when confronted with new problems will revert to private speech as they verbalise possible solutions.

The opposite of autonomy is heteronomy (control)

Piaget (1970) proposed that education should be for real life – the aim of which is autonomy, and well-adjusted individuals who function effectively in society. The autonomy continuum runs from:

CONSTRAINT $\longrightarrow$ COOPERATION

Adults who may reward and/or chastise particular behaviours do not support the development of autonomy; that is Constraint $\rightarrow$ Cooperation happens when all parties are involved in the construction of learning, when there are agreed values and behaviours in place, and in older boys the opportunity to self-assess and feel positive about themselves as learners and individuals.

Cooperation occurs on an 'equal footing', providing an atmosphere of respect and exchange of valued viewpoints which encourages participants to explain their reasoning to the other. Cooperation fosters autonomy because children use intelligence to work together in a search for sense; they become 'active researchers'. Morally and ethically they work together to determine what is right and wrong and accept responsibility.

Autonomy allows individuals to critically evaluate situations. The natural desire of children to figure out their world needs support and nurturing to assist their reasoning and independence, therefore enhancing the ability to act autonomously.

Supporting the development of autonomy

The security and sensitivity of adults fosters independent, curious and confident children. COOPERATION leads to pride and confidence. CONSTRAINT leads to worry, shame and doubt.

Deci (1975) suggested it is possible to provide limits without being controlling. Children are more likely to accept external processes into their own core value system if:

- the process is presented in a meaningful way
- the child's perspective is acknowledged
- there is an atmosphere of choice rather than control.

Under these conditions children view the feedback from adults as information that they can use for themselves rather than messages of control. The feedback provides support for autonomy while encouraging new ways to approach a task.

Negotiation helps children work out the sorts of issues that are within their own control – a 'co-operative relationship' (Piaget, 1970) between child and adult is vital to support autonomy.

Nucci, Killen and Smetana (1996) state that *'although teachers may view the facilitation of autonomy as an important goal of the pre-school classroom, it is likely that this goal is sub-ordinated to other goals such as maintaining order and fostering group activities'.*

Children need to participate in cooperative negotiation with adults to develop a sense of themselves as decision makers. Assuming authority over personal issues marks the beginning of accepting responsibility for decisions.

Research shows that it is between the ages of four and five that children show a firm sense of personal authority, that is, not just the *'because'* statements but rather a deeper understanding of *why*. For children to develop a confident understanding that they have the authority to make decisions over personal actions they need to experience a variety of social contexts at home and school.

Kamii (2006) researched the beneficial effects of autonomy, linking it to the supportive conditions and children's attainment in school. Autonomy is strongly related to performance, the Piagetian notion of cooperation and critical analysis of other children's reasoning leads to a greater understanding at a personal level and an 'ownership' of concepts.

The research of Gronlick and Ryan (1989) indicates that more autonomous children have greater classroom and social competence and are less likely to have behavioural difficulties. Autonomy in children leads to greater persistence, higher participation and curiosity about the world around them. Children who are 'externally controlled' report feelings of boredom, tedium, anxiety and frustration. The study concluded that supporting autonomy in children promotes an interest in continual learning.

The implications of this are that autonomy is supported when:

- children are free to make real choices that affect their lives
- adult/child relationships are characterised by cooperative negotiation
- children do not feel pressurised into behaving in pre-determined ways.

Providing real choices

Central to autonomy are children's perceptions that they have a legitimate decision-making authority in certain matters in their lives. Offering children choices has long been accepted practice in early years and is advocated as developmentally appropriate (Bredekamp and Copple 1997).

Research by Nucci, Killen and Smetana (1996) highlighted that practitioner's reactions to children proactively asserting their choices often do not include the vital negotiation component. The findings indicate that if practitioners were more able to exchange viewpoints with children rather than simply negating the unexpected choices, the children would develop a more secure sense of the issues that are within their decision-making authority.

The concept of choice needs to be extended to include the things children find important in their lives, such as friendship. We have all heard the practitioner use the statement 'We're all friends here' in order to promote pro-social behaviours. However, friendship is a very mutual and exclusive relationship, not a collection of pro-social behaviours. By the practitioner proclaiming universal friendship, the child's choice of whether to participate in such relationships is eliminated, the statement becomes an external control and the degree of cooperation within the relationship is reduced.

Helping children realise that they can 'choose' friends encourages them to discover more about different people, discovering the qualities that they find valuable in a relationship. Choosing friends is an autonomous choice that leads to greater cooperation.

Providing informal not controlling limits

Young boys need structure in their environment; it makes them feel safe to know where the boundaries are. However, it is the manner in which these boundaries are communicated that makes a vast difference to children's own perceptions of their autonomy and consequently their school attainment (Koestner 2008).

Vocabulary such as *should, must, have to*, conveys a message that is detrimental to autonomous action. I would, however, caveat this by stating that adult-initiated challenge, shared with children can result in some 'challenges' that the children will need to do during the course of the day or week. This is independent autonomous thought, there are some jobs that I need to do – when I do them – well, that is down to me. So limits can be used that may actually enhance intrinsic motivation, as long as they are communicated in an uncontrolling manner and include a meaningful rationale.

Research shows that the traditional unilateral model of teaching interferes with the development of autonomy. Kamii (2006) suggests that practitioners promote more mutuality by exchanging points of view with children which helps the children realise that their views are important. Consequently the interaction becomes more cooperative and supportive of autonomous action. Such an attitude of mind promotes ownership within the setting and awareness that problems that arise are not the sole responsibility of the adult (Strachota, 1996).

Children should also be involved in decision making such as determining which topics or themes to follow, allowing the curriculum to become emergent. Showing an interest in the children's ideas shows a respect for the children's intrinsic motivation. Under these circumstances the children are likely to develop an ownership of their learning, promoting deep-level learning. The most effective use of an emergent curriculum approach is when the adult and children actively wonder together and share the responsibility for planning possibilities.

To conclude, it is important that adults too experience real choices. We all operate within parameters that are specific to our situation. However, within these parameters we can make autonomous decisions about the education of the children within our setting. The choices we make reflect our core value structure, and each practitioner must make an autonomous decision about whether or not enhancing children's autonomy fits in with theirs.

Autonomy and problem solving in action – an observation

A group of nursery-aged boys were digging a hole. It was a big hole, so big that they could actually stand knee deep in it. The boys had proper equipment with which to dig the hole – big shovels, a big fork, hard hats and high visibility jackets. The boys had selected this activity, it was not on the plan as a learning aim 'to dig an enormous great hole'. They had located the correct equipment from the garden shed and they had been digging for at least half an hour, taking turns to chip away at the clay and chalk.

The boys decided that the purpose of the hole was to fill it with water and float stuff on it. They needed something to carry the water in. What was available? The boys spied some buckets so they took them to the outdoor tap and promptly started to fill them up. However, there was a problem, the buckets were too heavy for one person to carry so they had to team up to carry them – they were still too heavy and a lot of water was being spilt in transit.

What could they do? The boys decided to fill the buckets 'half way' to ease carrying.

Another problem, the water didn't stay in the hole, it 'magicked away all the time' so no water was staying in the hole.

This was a big problem to solve so they approached an adult and explained the situation. The adult suggested that they might want to find something that went straight into the hole from the tap. The boys thought about this for a while and then had a 'eureka' moment – 'the hose, the hose, let's use the hose'. They asked the adult if she could help to put the hose on the tap.

Then there was another problem – the hose was not long enough to reach the hole.

What could they do? The boys didn't want to use the buckets again, so they scoured the nursery to find another means of transporting the water. Exploration of the shed revealed some lengths of guttering – 'We can use this'.

And so they did – they placed the hose into the guttering and positioned the guttering towards the hole. On went the tap, the hole filled with water, bits of flotsam were thrown in to see if they would float – job done!

This was true autonomy and problem solving in action, and because the practitioner facilitated rather than dominated the thinking process, real deep-level learning took place.

'The pleasure of learning and knowing, and of understanding, is one of the most important and basic feelings that every child expects from the experiences he confronts alone, with other children or with adults. It is a crucial feeling which must be reinforced so that the pleasure survives even when reality may prove that learning, knowing and understanding involve difficulty and effort.'

Loris Malaguzzi

Getting it right for boys

Facilitative qualities

Let us now look at what Carl Rogers (1969) calls these adult 'Facilitative Qualities'. Roger's perspective was:

- The behaviour adults display towards children affects the learning process.
- Adults who provide children with autonomy are more effective educators.
- Adults who empathise with children and who are sensitive to children's emotional well-being are more effective educators.

Rogers looked at three qualities in particular:

1. Genuineness – when the practitioner is not presenting a façade. Children are very quick at spotting adults who are not being genuine. These are the adults who are usually left alone at the play dough table or in the role play. Children spot these charlatans a mile away, they have the capacity to empty a room of children before you can say 'Whatever next!'
2. Caring – where there is acceptance and trust, the adult values and trusts the child as an individual in their own right, and the adult shows sensitivity for a child's concerns.
3. Understanding – when the practitioner understands the learner's actions from the inside, they know their children and fully understand the individual thought and behavioural processes taking place.

Rogers' work concluded that in settings where the above were displayed there was more:

- talk initiated by children
- problem solving (again that link to creative thinkers)
- questioning of the status quo
- involvement by the children in planning their own learning and assessing it
- eye contact
- higher levels of cognition
- creativity.

Stimulation

As early years practitioners our role as 'players' and co-researchers in young children's lives and learning is vital. A recent research project in Croydon (2010) (which focused on the role of the adults in early years settings and schools) revealed that while adults were authentic in their sensitivity towards children and children's concerns, there was a lack of genuine stimulation. That is to say, too many adults were not engaging with the needs, fascinations and interests of the children, boys in particular, and using them to stimulate, promote, excite, and further the learning possibilities.

This is a two-tier issue:

- Adults as role models for playing and learning
- Validating and extending learning contexts

Laevers (1994) defines stimulation as *'the way in which the adult intervenes in the learning process and the content of such interactions'*.

Can you become a stimulating person? How stimulating are you? Young children learn though watching and imitation – if they see an active, open-minded, enquiring and stimulating person the chances are that you will inspire them to be likewise. Conversely, if the children are with an adult who is bored, unquestioning and lacking in stimulation – not only is that person in the wrong job, but they are also profoundly damaging children's potential.

The three-way model for effective learning and teaching

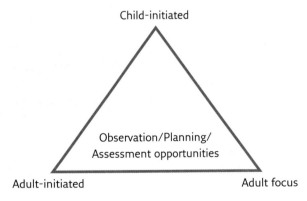

Child-initiated

Observation/Planning/
Assessment opportunities

Adult-initiated   Adult focus

Getting it right for boys

Effective supportive practitioners for boys take into consideration these three elements of learning, there is a mixture of the taught and the initiated. It all feeds back into the planning cycle. Good learning and teaching is a mixture of:

- What you see
- What the boys need
- How are you going to deliver?

The learning continuum – stick in the MIDDLE!

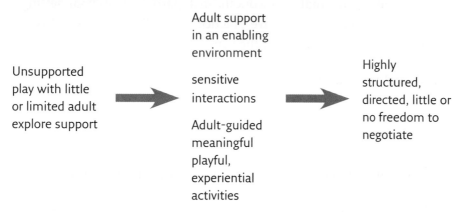

Unsupported play with little or limited adult explore support → Adult support in an enabling environment sensitive interactions Adult-guided meaningful playful, experiential activities → Highly structured, directed, little or no freedom to negotiate

If we allow boys total freedom in the guise of 'autonomy' we are failing them. Unstructured repetitive play soon breaks down if there is limited adult support and we are back at stage one – the self-fulfilling prophesy of boys not being able to concentrate and so becoming a 'problem'. Conversely, if we totally regulate boys' behaviour and give them highly structured play or little room for experimentation then we are damaging the potential to learn.

Excellent practitioners are in the middle. They provide a mixture of adult tasks (deployed in a playful meaningful way) that stretch and enthuse boys along with self-initiated learning in which the adult intervenes, observes and extends. Learning becomes fun!

Reflecting on practice

Consider the following questions in relation to your setting:

- Do all practitioners feel that they know the boys in their key groups – what can be done to improve this?
- Does your setting evaluate developing relationships between practitioners and parents of boys?
- Do families and practitioners truly value the choices that boys make?
- Do you encourage males to work in/visit/participate in your setting?
- Do you have not only 'Creative Practice' but a 'Practice which fosters Creativity?' – the two are not the same.

Ensure that you do the following:

- Encourage greater self-motivation, empathy, reflection, optimism and self-awareness of boys about themselves and others.
- Place greater emphasis on speaking and listening.
- Allow time for review of learning; give boys the opportunity to be more reflective of their achievements.
- Ensure boys are motivated and interested – they *will not* work if they do not see the point!
- Ensure that adults act as researchers and learning takes a personal path based upon the individuality of the child.
- Consider what curriculum you have on offer for your boys. Is it engaging interests or is it negating them?

As a leader in a school or setting you must question how adults support the boys in your setting. Consistency of approach is vital. Do all practitioners share the same value system and vision for boys' learning? Do they value the physical, the boisterous, the being slightly out of control, the rough and tumble and the sheer wonderment at being able to run scream, shout and be themselves?

4 The physical and emotional environment

We cannot and must not separate the physical and emotional environments – they are linked inextricably. Get the physical environment right, have age appropriate resources and expectations and you will have emotionally secure children who can get on with the busy process of learning about learning and thinking about thinking.

It is interesting that the latest review of the Early Years Foundation Stage (2012) highlights Physical Development and the Personal and Social aspects of learning as 'Prime Areas'.

Owning the learning environment

Anthony Eden wrote, *'Man should be master of his environment, not its slave. That is what freedom means'* (1960). Does the environment make the person or does the person construct the environment? Are you allowing the boys in your settings to make influential and autonomous decisions about their learning environment – both the physical environment and the emotional environment?

As we have discussed, boys need to have ownership of the learning environment and they need to feel part of the process in constructing that environment. If they are constantly 'done to' they will have little or no emotional engagement with the environment or the learning it may or may not offer. Without an emotional connection or response to any given learning opportunity, the learning and the links between learning will be non-existent or at best extremely patchy.

Think of the boys in your setting, do they 'own' the environment or are they ruled by its constraints and routines? These are constraints and routines that are too often adult driven and which are based upon adult needs and adult belief systems of how young children learn. They are routines which are put in place to underpin the authority of the adult.

For many young boys, movement and freedom to move is as vital as air. Movement is, in essence, thought in action. How many action words do you use to describe thought:

- jump to it
- trip over an issue
- throw my lot in
- get a balance of things – and so on.

We do it all the time and what boys are doing in their physical play is putting thought into action. Without doubt, movement, muscles and thought are entwined. Think how boys learn, the physicality, the rough and tumble, the knowing when to stop, the practice of barriers – boys bond with others and their environments through running, action and tumble play.

Why is this so important? Well here's some more brain development. The part of the brain that we are most concerned about here is the hippocampus. It belongs to the limbic system and plays important roles in the consolidation of information from short-term memory to long-term memory, spatial navigation and the emotional links to learning. If the hippocampus is under stress or duress it actually shrinks in size and releases chemical toxins into the brain. We have to keep this little engine happy by ensuring the emotional and physical environments are meeting its needs.

The politics of learning

I would urge you strongly to look at your environments, as they will undoubtedly reflect your own views on learning – are children passive recipients or active participants? It begs the question: *What are your politics of learning?*

For more than 300 years the idea that nurture is the determining factor in human actions has been used to argue for a variety of social programmes. If we can only change people's environments, the argument

Getting it right for boys

goes, we can make a better humanity, reduce crime, fight poverty and get rid of the gender difference in education. This creed is usually associated with the politics of the Left. On the other hand, if you believe nature is responsible for much of what we are, heavily influencing such things as intelligence, personality traits, perhaps even propensity to commit crimes, then there are limits to what social programmes and educational philosophies can do to reduce the individual differences between people. This conviction is often thought to fit better with the politics of the Right.

This debate is as old as the hills, but yet it still influences the way practitioners interact with children and the expectations they have of them. Are there underlying traits that nullify a more nurturing approach to learning, or are these traits more societal expectation rather than biological fact? We know that boys have a different chemical make-up from girls, that they employ different learning styles and prefer a more tactile experiential way of learning – these are biological facts. Best practice is to nurture these traits into worthwhile experiences, to harness them into an inclusive learning philosophy that recognises differences and celebrates them, so bringing together similarities in learning opportunities, but differentiating the methods and expectations of getting there.

If you are of the opinion that boys will always be the same regardless, that they are boys, they are what they are, and we should expect nothing less or more of them, then it is time to re-evaluate your stance on educational theory and practice. Boys will be boys, that is a given, it is because that is what they are! It is how you nurture that boy, that self-belief, that willingness to try things out, that separates the adequate from the outstanding. The *Researching Effective Pedagogy in the Early Years* (REPEY) study (Siraj-Blatchford et al. 2002) stated that it is the importance and effectiveness of the adult/child relationships that are the key indicators of quality within the most effective settings.

In March of 2005, the cover story for *Time* magazine included this statement: '*Until recently, there have been two groups of people: those who argue sex differences are innate and should be embraced and those who insist that they are learned and should be eliminated by changing the environment. Sax is one of the few in the middle – convinced that boys and*

girls are innately different and that we must change the environment so differences don't become limitations.'

I believe this is the way forward. We all know that all children are different, that is why good practitioners do what they do so well and so instinctively, they note differences and act accordingly. The cohort you have affects your environment, both physically and emotionally and constant review of how children are utilising your enabling environment is the sign of outstanding practice.

The physical and emotional atmosphere in the learning place must be good, or, in short, the ethereal 'vibe' it gives off must be good for learning. *'An appropriate environment is key both to safety and to effective learning and development.'* (DfES 2007).

The emotional environment

This consists of knowledgeable adults who children trust and who observe and respond to their needs. These are essential parts of both the learning and emotional environment.

These adults should:

- offer a range of experiences and resources which are regularly monitored and refreshed to keep them safe and stimulating
- tune in to the children's interests and interact with them to support and extend their learning and development, jointly engaging in problem solving and sustained shared thinking
- respond to observed interests and plan new materials and experiences within the environment that reflect these
- monitor materials, children's involvement and their own involvement with children to ensure they offer relevant experiences
- provide materials that reflect diversity in order to avoid stereotypical images or approaches
- evaluate their provision to ensure that everything that is provided is of the highest quality.

Getting it right for boys

Outdoor and indoor environments

The outdoor and indoor environments should contain resources and materials that children can explore and investigate using all their senses. Some of the materials and resources should be familiar to the children from their home and community environments, and some should be new. The best materials will have many uses, such as wooden hoops and pegs in a tin, cardboard boxes, rope and planks of wood. They will provide unlimited opportunities for children to use them creatively and imaginatively to support their learning and development.

Five factors that contribute to a good learning environment

1. Motivation is perhaps the most important factor in any learning environment. First and foremost, boys must be highly motivated to learn. Motivation will be the driving force that makes boys stick with it even when they are having trouble understanding the information being presented to them during the session. Indeed, any problem with learning can be overcome if the child's motivation is high enough. The key question is – *How do we motivate children?*
    - By following interests and incorporating interests in planning and provision.
    - By acting as a mediator in the learning experience.
    - Through meaningful and challenging experiences.

2. But just as important, the practitioner must also be highly motivated to teach, for that is what you are doing, even for the youngest of children. They will watch you, trust you, and imitate you. You are teaching them and modelling for them experiences and behaviours that they do not know. So you need to get your behaviour right – all of the time. Practitioners must have a burning desire to relate information and learning during sessions in a way that all children can access and understand, especially boys.

    When boys in your setting are having problems, are the

practitioners motivated enough to spend the extra time it takes to ensure that the problem is resolved? Do they make sure that the boys understand the requirements and expectations of the setting and the challenges it may offer both physically and emotionally?

3. I quite like the American term 'aptitude'. This will determine how quickly and easily learning will be for the boys in your setting. The aptitude of the skilled practitioner to work alongside the children will contribute to determining how quickly and easily children feel positive about themselves as learners and catch on to new initiatives and themes. This might involve designing and making attention-holding environments and displays, giving pertinent meaningful analogies and stories, preparing illustrative visuals, designing realistic practice exercises for children to develop skills and knowledge in a safe and caring environment, and in general, keeping the children's involvement level high.

    Practitioners with high aptitude make it easy for children to learn. There is a symbiotic relationship between the engaged adult and the involved child. If the adult is more engaged the child will be more involved and the more a child is involved the greater will be the adult engagement in the learning process.

4. Presentation and the environment is at the heart of learning and enjoyment. Here's a simple task. Think about where you like to go shopping, or out for an evening, lunch and so on. Compile a simple table:

Where do I like to go?	Why – what is the selling point?	Does my setting reflect this thinking?
'Excellent Mart'	Clean displays Colourful displays Access good Helpful staff Wide aisles Good selection of produce Interesting articles to buy	THIS IS THE KEY QUESTION – given the choice would you attend the setting or would you look elsewhere for environments that meet your physical and emotional needs

Why do you go to particular places – do they make you feel good about yourself? Are the staff helpful? Is there a high quality range of goods? Are they affordable? There are so many questions, but these are questions you must be asking of your setting. You invariably go to certain places for a plethora of reasons but the underlying one is that of *quality.* Quality can only be defined by reflection and contrast as Pirsig (1984) wrote, '*Quality is neither mind nor matter, but a third entity independent of the two, even though quality cannot be defined you know what it is'.*

The best practitioners and settings prepare and deliver the environment as a presentation and representation of their own values, and it is then easier for children to feel emotionally safe and for the learning to take place.

5. Practice with reinforcement acts as the gauge to judge the success of an enabling environment. Well-planned practice, application and ongoing learning opportunities should be realistic and meaningful, based upon children's fascinations and interests.

With boys this might well entail superhero or weapon play. Boys like to be these characters and we cannot ignore popular culture, it surrounds us at every turn. As practitioners we cannot avoid the influences of the media, but how should we respond? All children are affected by media influences, just as we are. We need to be aware of how this happens and the messages that children are receiving. I like to joke about it at training but part of your research and job is to watch children's television, the cartoon network, the comics and books that are current fascinations – what are they saying? What behaviour are they portraying?

Superhero and weapon play is a common theme for many young boys, and some girls, so we, as professionals, need to be aware of why children want to play in this way. Superheroes often, but not always, carry some sort of weapon, to use in times of emergency. This should force settings and practitioners to be clear about their policy regarding superhero play. Too often settings choose to ban it completely, the amount of times I have heard, '*No thank you, we don't play that here'* is innumerable.

Here's a tale of pirate play

I was doing an observation of a reception class and the theme was pirates. Excellent I thought, how exciting: lots of language, physical play and the opportunity to become immersed in the role of a pirate. To my dismay I soon discovered that these pirates were not allowed to have swords of any variety. Talk about taking away the context of learning – pirates have swords, it's what they do best!

During the observation, I happened across a group of young buccaneers in the outdoor environment, and guess what? They were sword fighting. They had made swords out of construction bricks, old pieces of wood and whatever they could lay their hands on. There was much discussion about different types of swords, which was the 'bestest one' and how the game would evolve – so language-rich it was.

The buccaneers then spotted me, and realising that sword play was not condoned, one of the pirates, complete with eye patch and hat turned to me and said, 'It's alright we are hoovering the garden' and promptly started to demonstrate his best shake and vac action. It was a genius moment and I was bowled over by the quick thinking – however what I was most concerned about was the fact that the boys had to compromise their play for the sake of adult regulations in the emotional environment.

Superhero and weapon play

What practitioners need to realise and analyse is what is going on behind the superficial play. In the modern age many children live in a gun culture. Think also of children whose parents are in the armed forces – *are guns bad, is my daddy or mummy bad?* Superhero and gun play often allow children to explore anxieties and issues about keeping safe and solving problems. If adults suppress this play, we are suppressing their thinking and are marginalising an opportunity to influence learning, thinking and behaviour.

Superhero play affords boys the opportunity to be boisterous and to run, and if we suppress it we will simply drive the play underground where it is deregulated and secretive. They will get the message that what they know something about, or are passionate about is not valued by the practitioners and adults in the setting. This is all part of creating an emotional environment in which children feel safe and secure to be that 'other' person. It is a sad fact that too many of the things that young boys are interested in are marginalised within their environments. What this never fails to do is reinforce the belief that learning for them is not relevant because they can never do what they like to do.

'Many practitioners do not value war, weapon and superhero play as a form of imaginative play. Many feel that its themes are simply dictated by films, video and TV series, which have limited and repetitive contents based crudely on a struggle between good and evil and thus offer children little in terms of extended imaginary play... A major difficulty with this analysis is that because children are generally interrupted in such play scenarios I do not feel that we can begin to evaluate the imaginative potential of such scenarios unless we allow them to develop.'

Penny Holland (2003)

The point here is that the majority of boys will indulge in weapon or superhero play, it is what they see and what they are surrounded by. Children will imitate play, and sensitive adults will engage in that play and add innovation and thought to it to move it forward so it does not become repetitive. Some children will, however, need to revisit play scenarios time and time again to assimilate play – again a key point for the emotional environment.

The intrepid duo – my brother and me (I am on the left) tooled up and ready for action.

Things to ponder upon

- Do you value the characters and personalities that are most influential on your boys?
- Do you discuss alternative way of doing things or do you stifle play with your own agenda and disapproval?
- Do you take the time to understand how boys might use this play as a means of exploring learning?
- Do you engage meaningfully in the play using narratives rather than questions?
- Do you provide safe ways for boys to use their energy and strength in positive ways?

In short – are you a radiator or a drain?

In my element as a toddler, outside, nice and warm – with a stick for digging – what an environment!

The above picture is of my brother and me in the early 1970s (we were fortunate to have fields at the back of the house – now taken over by housing!) We were playing war, note the fort my brother has made. The victim is my sister, and I have just been 'taken out'.

High challenge and low stress

The best learning environment, both emotionally and physically, is one which offers high challenge and low stress. Resources should be easily accessible, age appropriate and even more importantly, children should be allowed to access them at all times. Skillful practitioners will be very much aware of their children's stage of development, both physically and cognitively. The environment needs to mirror this development; you cannot fit a square peg into a round hole. If chronologically you have a

Getting it right for boys

group of boys who are three or four, but your observations, discussions and assessments have highlighted that they are operating at a two to three-year-old level, you will have to reassess the physical and emotional environment in order for it to be accessible, safe and meaningful for these particular children.

I have a saying when I am in nursery and reception classes, which often shocks practitioners and headteachers alike, '*You need to take the tables and chairs out and burn them*'. Now this might seem like a drastic and expensive course of action, but I ask you to think about your learning environment:

- Do you have a preponderance of chairs and tables? Why?
- Do you believe that good learning only happens when children are sitting at a table?

Think how young boys learn best: by movement, by lying on the floor, by transporting stuff around. They need *space* and lots of it, so I would urge you to look at the table and chair dynamic in your setting or classroom. Do they dominate, and if so, move them so the children have more space to lie on the floor, to spread out and to become connected by using their whole body. Boys need time for rough and tumble play, it is this play that teaches them self-control and that there is a point when you need to stop.

Unfortunately in a predominantly female working and learning environment many boys are told to stop before they are physically and emotionally ready to, which leads to a disharmony in the behaviour and ever-increasing stress levels. Remember the testosterone and the hippocampus! We do not want to penalise boys for behaving in a way that is natural to them.

Outdoor learning

If you are fortunate enough to have an immediate outdoor space, then it is your duty to ensure that children are out in it for prolonged periods of time, boys even more so. A good outdoor space is the perfect learning environment for many boys. It is big, there is fresh air, and the surface might even be slightly unlevelled (wow – how risky!). Boys often go through a chemical change when they are outdoors for prolonged periods –

endorphins are produced, there is a feel-good factor, fresh air in the lungs and rain on the face – enlivening! It was Margaret Macmillan who stated, *'The best classroom and the richest cupboard are roofed only by the sky.'* (1914)

Too often adult routines get in the way of prolonged outdoor learning. I recently visited a school, in a very disadvantaged area of North East London, where the routine was so inflexible the reception aged children only got 45 minutes outdoors every day. When you added in lining up (what is it with lining up in so many of our schools, and lining up in silence!), putting coats on and then taking them off, this equated to less than 35 minutes. To my mind that is criminal and is not catering for the physical, cognitive and emotional needs of the children in any shape or form. The *Start Active/ Stay Active* document released by the Chief Medical Officers of England, Scotland, Wales, and Northern Ireland in July 2011 strongly recommends that children are outside for a minimum of three hours a day to ensure physical and cognitive aspects of learning are developed sufficiently.

The outdoor environment should be full of *big* things, things to carry about, and things to get in. On too many occasions I have seen the outdoor environment merely mirroring what is going on indoors and often with the same resources. Tables and chairs outside with bits of A4 paper – what is all that about! Small sand and water trays – what on earth! Construction on tables – good grief! If you have sand outside it should be *big* so the children can *get in* the sand and feel it on their feet and hands. The water should be on a massive scale so children can experiment with flow and distribution and not worry if the water goes on the floor – using guttering, tubes, buckets and hosepipes. Relinquish some of that adult power and start to have fun!

The building site

There was a building site next to the school nursery and a seven foot fence had been erected to shield the site from the school. The practitioners were aware that many of the boys were becoming increasingly interested in the building site so together they designed their own, complete with delivery lorries and a builders' merchants for meaningful numeracy and writing opportunities. There were hard hats, high visibility jackets, goggles, gloves and magnificently, real tools, ladders and bricks.

The boys were having a great time in their imaginary world. The practitioner asked the builders for sand and they actually came into the setting to show off their plans and equipment. The learning was immeasurable, the boys were highly involved in planning projects, digging holes, mixing 'cement' and laying bricks. However, the noise of the building site was ever alluring for some of the boys and they would often try to peer through the fence to get a glimpse of the trucks and diggers – what to do?

One morning I observed a group of boys carrying a ladder to the fence and propping it up. There then followed a discussion on what to do next. Who was going to hold the ladder and who was going to climb it and have a look over the fence? Once this was decided Owen scrambled up the ladder with George and Dean holding the base. Owen then proceeded to regale his colleagues with the size of the diggers, the colours of them, the size of the houses and what the men were doing. What a fantastic learning experience – emotionally safe, secure, risk taking, problem solving, using language for thinking and language for communication. Very happy days indeed!

Consistency and variety

Boys do enjoy structure, so ritualised and patterned positive behaviour from a practitioner influences boys' dispositions hugely. Ensure your environment does have a structure, as without this many boys can feel emotionally lost, but keep this structure flexible and do not be driven by it. Boys enjoy constant and varied exposure to consistent and new exciting materials – just as we do in reality.

When we go to our favourite shop, we know the staples will be there but we also know that there may well be some new and exciting goodies available as well. It is extremely unlikely that the shop assistant will say to you, *'I know you like milk, but we had that out last week so we have something else this week'*. You would not be too impressed if this actually happened! Around the milk aisle in supermarkets they also have variants – yogurts, cheeses, crème fraiche, cream. This is exactly what needs to happen with your environment and provision – put the basics out but what else can you add to extend it? Keep the consistent provision, but add to it to extend the learning.

Learning strategies

A good environment encourages quicker and deeper learning. Children feel emotionally secure and are confident in making decisions, safe in the knowledge that those decisions will be encouraged and acted upon by sensitive adults. Sensitive and differentiated routines and expectations are necessary for effective individualised learning. Good practitioners employ a range of learning and teaching strategies within planning. They ensure resources are appropriate, accessible, identifiable and relevant to children's learning needs.

If you think back to the vision statement scenario in the introduction to this book (see page 11), your environment should support pupils to become independent and active learners. Children learn best through a mixture of physical and cognitive challenges. True active learning involves children being synonymous with and integral to planning. It involves other people, ideas and objects so I would strongly urge you to adopt a collaborative approach when planning for children's needs.

It is thought that a good visual display can improve recall and attention by up to 80 per cent. Displays must be interactive and not just about things that we have done. Nicely double-backed, sometimes triple-backed displays, arranged to look good, might do so to an adult. But children need ownership of displays, they are the children's, it is the children's property you are displaying. Let them have a say in what is being displayed and why (displays are ongoing) – this is what we are learning about, this is what we have found out and this is what we are going to find out.

A tale of paint mixing and expectation

When I started my teaching career in a nursery class I made myself a promise – I would never, and I mean never, make paints for children. I would engage them in the process, teach them a new skill and let them develop it with confidence. Initially this would involve ensuring that resources were accessible to all children at all times, they were conveniently positioned and clearly labelled and that it was alright for the children to take them out by themselves. Small groups of children were then taught the process of mixing paints. This was initially an adult-directed activity, then with adult mediation and then gradually all the children were capable and confident to do it independently.

To start with, as you can imagine it was a complete mess – we only used powder paint as this gives you texture (ready-mix is just cheating!) and consistency. But over time the confidence and competence grew. All you need are three pots of primary colours and white, (it invariably turns brown!) a water dispenser, pots and brushes to mix with. Now look at the learning opportunities and the emotional security that this environment has created.

Rowan decided he was going to do some painting on a particular day:

- Firstly he found an apron and put it on himself.
- He then located the paper store and decided on the colour, shape and size of the paper he was going to use.
- He used the grips to put his paper on the easel.
- He remembered he needed to write his name on the paper so he located his name card and a thick pencil and scribed his interpretation of his name on the front of the paper. It didn't matter that he would promptly paint over it!
- He then used a spoon to tip his chosen paints into his mixer, and added the required amount of water.
- He decided to use a thick brush and his fingers to paint with.
- On completion he took the picture down and placed it on the drying rack.
- He made a rudimentary attempt at washing his pot and brush and hung up his apron ready for his next slice of learning.

Rowan was three and a half years old.

Key considerations

Remember that the environment will have a huge impact on the children's limbic brain, the emotional response to learning. It is our duty and children's right to have the best possible early years' experience where they can safely imagine, create and experiment. The multi-sensory approach to developing your environment is a must.

There are some key considerations to be taken into account:

1 The visual environment – what does it look like?
2 The aural environment – noise levels and sounds.

3 The behavioural environment – expectations of adults and children – does the environment promote positive behaviour?

4 The internal environment – does it meet the needs of the children, emotionally, physically and cognitively – is it stimulating?

5 The external environment – does this extend and enhance the internal environment, does it allow for prolonged periods of physically active and cognitively-stimulating activity?

All five considerations should be part of your regular self-evaluation schedule. The table below is a useful planning and evaluation tool that you would need to work through with colleagues.

Enhancing the learning environment

Key element	Objective	Action
Visual	What is your aim?	How are you going to do it? Who is leading? How will you measure impact on learning?
Aural	What is your aim?	How are you going to do it? Who is leading? How will you measure impact on learning?
Behavioural	What is your aim?	How are you going to do it? Who is leading? How will you measure impact on learning?
Internal	What is your aim?	How are you going to do it? Who is leading? How will you measure impact on learning?
External	What is your aim?	How are you going to do it? Who is leading? How will you measure impact on learning?

The learning environment for adults

So far we have looked at the learning environments for the children – what about the adults? They too need a positive and relaxed physical and emotional environment in which to work, feel included, part of the team and appreciated. It is well worth working with your team on the following

Getting it right for boys

document and you might well find that the environments for children and adults are not too dissimilar.

It is pretty self-explanatory. List the necessary attributes and attitudes that will ensure an excellent and outstanding learning environment that is suitable for a range of learning styles:

Positive environment for learners	Postive environment for adults
Consistency of staff members	Could echo the previous column really!
Key people to support them	
Regular routines	
Consistency of approach to learning and teaching	
Suitable open-ended resources that are accessible	
Consistent expectations	
Being a part of the planning process – involvement in the journey – having a voice that is heard and recognised	
Being able to make independent decisions	

In order to create a positive learning environment we need to discuss *what personal qualities you need to exhibit* in order to do this on a regular basis. I would suggest that you go back to your vision and values statement (see page 11). What sort of adults do we want to be working with the children in order to inspire them? The format of the table below is a useful tool for managers and leaders to design individualised continual professional development programmes for team members that echo the agreed vision and values of the setting.

Personal quality (what would you like to see in staff members)	Definition – linked to your interpretation and your vision and values	How can this be achieved – What training and support is required to assist?

Get this right and you will allow the following to happen.

Joshua and the Beyblades

Joshua was in the nursery and he and the other boys were fascinated by Beyblades, the cartoon with spinning top battles. The catchphrase was: '1, 2, 3 let 'em rip!' Initially we allowed the boys to bring in their Beyblades from home to play with and act out the games. However, missing and broken Beyblades made this a decision that we had to re-consider as there were lots of tears around the nursery.

We were aware, however, that the boys still wanted to play the games, so we thought about how this could happen. We had talks with them about what makes a good Beyblade and what were the best materials to make them with as they needed a strong pointy corner to spin on. We exhausted all possibilities, nothing was sustainable and simple to construct or repair.

Or so we thought, until Joshua came across the Polydron kit (interlocking two-dimensional shapes that made three-dimensional shapes)! He then started to click various shapes together, until he constructed a four-sided pyramid. He could spin this wickedly on its point and soon the other boys were copying Joshua and busily constructing their own now that a workable template had been discovered.

Soon the boys were busy having their Beyblade battles, constructing Beyblades of differing sizes and colour patterns. The Beyblades had the habit of breaking upon collision so time was spent putting them back together again. Joshua was not too happy about this and went on the prowl to make his Beyblade unbreakable and the best of the lot.

He searched high and low for something to assist him and then he happened upon the play dough table. He sat there pondering for a while, picked up the play dough, opened his Beyblade and shoved the play dough inside. In doing so he created an extra-heavy machine that was also held together from the inside. Needless to say Joshua's Beyblade was the master of the table, it obliterated everything in sight. The game was afoot – how would the others respond?

What learning, what autonomy of action, independence of thought, creativity – all taking place because the environment was secure and his decisions and thought processes were valued by adults.

Natural materials – the creation of creativity

In the previous chapters I noted that if we want our boys to achieve their true potential, we need to have settings and schools that do not just have 'creative practice' (whatever that actually means) but have a genuine desire to have a practice that actually fosters creativity. Creativity in its true sense is ensuring that children *think* about thinking; that they have the ability and disposition to actively create something out of something else to represent something that they do not have.

We have already discussed the link between the physical and cognitive, how neither can be developed in isolation of the other. We have also discovered that boys, generally, develop physically and emotionally later than girls. Consequently, there is growing concern about children spending too much time sitting indoors instead of playing outdoors. Recently focus has been on how the natural environment affords possibilities and challenges for children to explore their own abilities for exercise and overcoming problems. Studies have shown how children's play in the natural environment not only stimulates their physical fitness and 'connectiveness' but also their dispositions, social aspects of learning and imagination. There are also other benefits for children through developing their linguistic and conceptual skills in a meaningful context, and enhancing their spatial perception by seeing and interacting with real items in real time.

I am also fascinated by the American psychologist James Jerome Gibson, who was influential in changing the way we consider visual perception. According to his theory (1977), perception of the environment inevitably leads to some course of action. Affordances, or clues in the environment that indicate possibilities for action, are perceived in a direct, immediate way with no sensory processing. What this means is the open-endedness of your environment – what learning opportunities is it 'affording' the children, in the long term, in the short term and in the realms of physical, cognitive and emotional development?

A few years ago I was fortunate to attend a series of lectures by Ingunn Fjortoft from Telemark University College on the strengths of outdoor natural play on children's overall development. I was especially interested in this and how it related to boys.

An experimental study was carried out with five-year-old and six-year-old pre-primary school children. The experimental group was given the opportunity to learn through playing in the natural environment. The physical landscape, vegetation, and topography were the arena for activities and free play. The experimental group visited the arena two to three hours every day without fail, regardless of weather conditions. The reference group participated in normal kindergarten activities but visited the natural environment only occasionally.

The study lasted for nine months. The groups were measured before and after the implementation of the study utilising the Eurofit Motor Fitness Test - this is a set of nine physical fitness tests covering flexibility, speed, endurance and strength. The standardised test battery was devised by the Council of Europe for children of school age and has been used in many European schools since 1988. The series of tests are designed so that they can be performed within 35 to 40 minutes, using very simple equipment.

The results were startling: they showed a vast improvement in motor fitness in the experimental group compared to the reference group. Significant differences were found in coordination, balance skills and agility. It was also noticed that the amount of free play in the experimental group increased. There was also a considerable increase in the children's interest in and knowledge of nature.

The inevitable conclusion: by playing and utilising activities in the natural environment the children's motor fitness is improved. Nature affords possibilities and challenges for the children to explore their own abilities. The children feel more comfortable by being in the natural environment and their knowledge about nature increases. The study indicated that the natural environment is a stimulating arena for mastering and learning processes in pre-primary school children.

The theory of affordances in operation – my son at three 'fishing' by the river utilising branches, leaves and string!

Getting it right for boys

Checklist for your environment

To conclude, it is worth looking in depth at your physical and emotional environments – they underpin your philosophy and understanding of how young boys learn. Good learning happens through engagement and involvement and through the support of sensitive and knowledgeable adults who are willing to risk take, problem solve and make decisions.

A last checklist for your environment and some reasons to spend time on it!

Does it allow for vestibular activity?	Boys need to move! Opportunities for movement and balance should be in evidence in the environment. Include jumpolenes, indoor trampolines, water trampolines or backyard bouncers, swings and swing sets, rocking toys, ride-on toys, scooter boards, dance and motion, roller coasters, glider rockers, seesaws, teeter totters and therapy balls.
Does it cater for proprioceptive activity?	The term proprioception refers to a sense of joint position and body awareness, a sense of self. Pushing, pulling, lifting, digging and resistance work all support this. Ensure boys can transport items around the setting.
Does it support developing upper arm and shoulder strength?	Include monkey bars, climbing robes, pulling and pully systems – precursors to fine motor development.
Does it support cross lateral movement?	Provide opportunities for dancing, movements across the body and linking the hemispheres in the brain – get out the Barry White and start to boogey!
Does it provide experiences for hands and feet?	Ensure there are uneven surfaces to help practise balance, coordination and confidence. Allow children sensory experiences, such as taking shoes off to play in the sand and the water. Provide opportunities for moving and handling, for dexterous development.
Is your setting highly active?	Reduce sedentary learning by taking away the constraints – are practitioners aware of the age plus two rule (see page 38) and children's physical development requirements that impinge drastically on concentration and motivation?
Does your setting allow for rest and sleep?	Being a young boy is exhausting, physically, emotionally and cognitively. Ensure there are 'down periods' when children can have a 'rest'. Also realise that adults also require periods of solitude, introspection and reflection during the working day.
What training does your setting require?	The pervasive nature of physical learning and its impact on children's emotional well-being.
What is your policy and culture?	Revisit your vision and values constantly – they underpin everything you do.

Case studies

I am indebted to a number of schools and settings who have given me the time to observe fantastic practice, talk with skillful practitioners and watch boys becoming fully engaged in meaningful activities because the environment, the support from the adults and the level of challenge and expectation is pitched correctly.

I have also spoken to mums and dads on what they do with their boys, how they differ in behaviour and interest from their female siblings, especially in terms of concentration and movement. To many parents the difference is immediately apparent, it is not a matter of social conditioning or expectation, just the simple fact that their sons respond and act differently to their daughters, *'He's always on the go, never stops, here there and everywhere. She was very different and would concentrate at things for a long time, he flits all over the place'.* This is a very common response from the majority of parents when talking about their children.

An outstanding school

I have spent many hours in St Marys' Infant School in Croydon. This is an outstanding school with a clear vision of what makes good learning and teaching for all children. The school is in an area of severe deprivation and has an intake of 90 per cent of families with English as an Additional Language. However, all the children do achieve exceptionally well.

The reasons for this are complex and part of the DNA of the school. The school motto is *'Learning to love, loving to learn'* and this is apparent from the nursery through to Year 2. The philosophy for learning and teaching remains the same, so children and families are secure in the environment, the routines and the increasing expectations.

The school maps its curriculum around the needs and requirements of the children and their families. There is tremendous emphasis laid on

Getting it right for boys

the partnership between home and school so that together the children's learning journey can be continued in a stress-free loving environment. Children are encouraged to do their best and value the efforts of others. The head teacher calls this *'being kind'*, a very simple term but one that encapsulates so many traits, expectations, and beliefs – it is a unique place.

There is a whole-school awareness of gender differences, on learning styles, on entry data, progress, teaching and interaction methodologies. There is also a whole-school behaviour policy that is created by staff and children and that promotes kindness, respect and self-control. The key is that all parties are involved in the creation of documentation, especially the children, and in this case the boys.

The school employs lots of PSHE. The children understand the terms of the policy and understand how the rules improve their lives at school. This has been particularly beneficial for the boys as often they need a clear set of rules and expectations which they have ownership over and they need to have ownership over the consequences as well. The focus is on young children understanding that behaviour has consequences, for example, if we are kind to other people then we all have fun, are trusted and people want to play with us. If we are unkind then we cannot be trusted and people will not want to play with us.

Learning and teaching in the school is embedded in active learning. This assists in recognising and catering for a range of learning styles and interests. It actively encourages and allows the children to choose ways of learning that suit them and the tasks best, so that they become owners of the learning experience.

Here are a couple of observations from the school:

Case study 1

Boy A finds sitting and listening hard, is very wriggly and spends a great deal of time wandering, flitting from activity to activity and not engaging with learning or with other children or adults. The early years team find it very hard to document his learning. His learning journey record for evidence towards the profile is looking rather empty.

Case study 2

Boy B is very sociable but unfocussed and is constantly engaging in very boisterous play-fighting. He often finds himself in trouble, particularly at lunchtimes and doesn't seem to engage in learning activities.

Following discussion between key workers, parents and colleagues there was a general feeling among all the interested parties that these boys were not happy in the environment and consequently not learning effectively.

Action

- Extended observations of both children, taken at regular times during the day, showed that although it seemed that they were not engaging in any learning they did in fact enjoy activities which involved lots of movement. Boy A enjoyed building using the large bricks and tyres but often moved away when other children 'took over'. Boy B enjoyed ball play, climbing and was actually eager to do this with other children. He had, however, gained a reputation between his peers of being boisterous and the other children tended to back away leaving him quite isolated.
- In both cases the staff began to sensitively and discreetly intervene in the boys' play.

With Boy A they introduced a building site with house bricks, cement and so on, and made it a hard-hat area. They gave boy A the task of leading the building team to build a shed for keeping the sand toys safe and dry at night. This gave boy A a way to interact with the other children and to be actively engaged in learning, doing something he enjoyed and felt successful at. During his year in Reception he went on to be involved in a number of building projects, including building a jungle in the shed and a cave for a life-sized bear. He was not always in charge of the projects as after he had found a way in with the children he was happy to work cooperatively.

With boy B, they ensured that there were always active games for him to play. At first they had to intervene to sort out disputes and they

Getting it right for boys

had to ensure that there were clear rules for the games. Eventually, as boy B came to realise that the rules helped him to enjoy the game and ensured the other children stayed and played the games, less and less intervention was needed and he and the other children were able to invent their own rules.

As you can imagine, all these activities involved the boys in all six areas of learning at a progressively higher level.

Both boys went on to have a very successful time in EYFS and are now in Year 2 and predicted to achieve high level 2s. They are lively, active, happy and successful learners.

What had happened?

Through detailed dialogue and observations the team had worked together to ensure the boys received an exciting and stimulating set of learning experiences that were in line with actual levels of development and interests. Around this was a set of frameworks regarding expectation and behaviour. Boys do like structure and routines. Within this they can operate freely but without it they often become lost, stressed and agitated. This links to the previous chapters – if practitioners have in place stimulating, challenging, and enabling environments and a desire to fully pursue lines of inquiry with an open mind the learning potential is limitless.

Don't be constrained by the weekly plan, think bigger and reflect constantly. Ask simple questions, *'What went well today, how can we extend that tomorrow?'* to help you realise the full potential of all children. Use the innate energy and fascinations of the children to drive the practice – develop an agreed value system and pedagogy. Involve parents and families and bring the 'fun' back into learning.

Excuse me!

Daniel is a three-year-old, he is a typical boy, adventurous, sensitive, loving and active – he will have a go at anything. He has the most understanding and loving elder sister who placates him, looks after him, and sometimes gets annoyed with him – but such is family life!

He is a very polite little chap – when he requires adult attention he pipes up, 'Excuse me' and then asks for whatever it is he requires you to do. Daniel is a transporter, he moves things about everywhere. He has a myriad of projects running simultaneously and moves effortlessly between them, picking up on his play and extending it by adding new objects and initiatives to it.

Watching Daniel is exhausting, the physical and mental energy that goes into his 'work' is frightening. He is unafraid to take risks, he constantly problem solves by moving objects around and can sustain attention for prolonged periods of time. Daniel is very aware of the expectations of the house and is secure in them because he has been part of the process in developing them – they were not imposed on him, but rather developmentally incremented as his understanding moved forward.

Daniel adores adult company, but adults who are on his wavelength, those adults who are fun and he can laugh with and at, and who allow him equal partnership in his games. Only recently I observed Daniel playing with an adult at a barbecue. Daniel had watched a programme on the TV similar to Gladiators and wanted to 'run the gauntlet'. It was a simple concept, Daniel would run along the back of the garden while the adult would *gently* throw soft balls in his direction – the idea being that Daniel would dodge them and make his way safely across the garden.

It was a great game and a couple of times the ball would hit Daniel as he scarpered across the garden. He was loving it, 'Again, again!' (the typical refrain of a three-year-old). The adult was exhausted at the end, but what fun had been had, building of relationships, ownership of the game, making rules, physical development, dexterity and muscle training by the boat load. There was also lots of language development as the conversations Daniel had with the adult over the rules became more complex as other initiatives were brought into the game.

This is what young male learners do all the time. As practitioners you need to understand the needs of young male learners to take risks, to problem solve, to watch others, to negotiate and adapt. By doing so it will assist in changing mind-sets and help you to recognise where real learning is taking place.

The work of Sally Goddard Blythe (2009) is of paramount importance here: the need for boys to be physically active, to join up the hemispheres

Getting it right for boys

of the brain, to move across the centre line, to become joined up and capable of moving on in learning.

Male role models

As I've previously mentioned, it is a sad but undeniable fact that the early years and infant education is a very female dominated industry, and some boys may not see a positive male role model in their lives until the junior or sometimes secondary school.

Many schools and settings work incredibly hard to bring males into their environments so that boys can see men reading, writing, talking, laughing, joking and taking a keen and real interest in them as individuals.

I undertook a project with a number of settings to research the effect of positive male role models on boys' learning and development within the settings' environment. The outcomes of the project were simple – would boys be more engaged in meaningful learning if there were males to support them at chosen activities? As quantitive and qualitative measures I utilised the Laevers Involvement Schedules (1994).

Involvement signals

- **Concentration**
  Attention solely directed at activity.
- **Energy**
  Investment of a lot of energy, child is eager and stimulated.
- **Complexity and creativity**
  Child is working at the very edge of their capabilities and able to exhibit individuality in the activity.
- **Facial expression and posture**
  Posture can reveal high concentration or boredom, possible to distinguish between 'empty dreamy eyes' and 'intense' eyes.
- **Persistence**
  Duration of concentration at an activity, wanting to continue the satisfaction so prepared to put in effort to prolong it.

- **Precision**
  Attention to detail.
- **Reaction Time**
  Involved children are alert and react quickly to stimuli.
- **Language**
  Language used shows importance of activity.
- **Satisfaction**
  Pleased with what they have done and achieved.

Involvement scale description

- **Level 1 (low activity)**
  Simple, stereotypical, repetitive and passive activity. There is no energy and an absence of cognitive demand. The child might stare into space. NB – this could be a sign of inner concentration.
- **Level 2 (frequently interrupted activity)**
  Child is engaged but for 50 per cent of time shows non-activity. There may be frequent interruptions in the child's concentration, but involvement is not enough to return to the initial activity.
- **Level 3 (mainly continuous activity)**
  Child is busy but at a routine level, real signs of involvement are missing. There is some progress but energy is lacking and concentration is at a routine level. The child can be easily distracted.
- **Level 4 (continuous activity with intense moments)**
  Intense moments, resumed after interruptions. External stimuli cannot seduce the child away from their chosen activity.
- **Level 5 (sustained intense activity)**
  Child shows sustained intense activity revealing greatest involvement. In the observed period not all the signals need to be observed, but essential ones must be present – CONCENTRATION, CREATIVITY, ENERGY and PERSISTENCE.

The Involvement signals are physical and mental representations of learning. The involved person is investing vast amounts of physical and cognitive energy in a chosen activity and working at the very limit of their ability – they display in various degrees the signals noted above. The point with true involvement is that it allows for deep-level thinking to

Getting it right for boys

take place. There is a symbiotic relationship between involved children and truly engaging and well-meaning adults. The more involved a child is, because the emotional, physical and cognitive challenges are pitched at the right level, the more likely it is that the adult will become more engaged in the learning. Likewise when an adult makes a child feel comfortable about themselves, values their opinions and decisions and supports them in a sensitive and stimulating way, the more involved that child will become in the learning process.

I asked practitioners to target a sample number of boys in their settings and make a series of five two-minute observations on them over the course of a couple of days, focusing on the signals, the levels of Involvement and the learning they were undertaking.

If you are not yet using these scales to improve the quality of provision in your settings, I strongly urge that you do think about doing so as the impact they have on the received curriculum is outstanding.

I also designed and distributed a simple questionnaire to all practitioners and parents of the settings. The results were interesting and are listed here as percentages:

Question	Certain	No idea	Not too sure
1. Do you know how the boys are learning in your setting?	20	25	55
2. Do you know how much child-initiated talk and dialogue is there?	24	19	57
3. Do you know what play opportunities are there?	55	10	35
4. Do you know who participates in the play?	45	20	35
5. Do you know how creativity, imagination and choice are supported and fostered in the children?	20	45	35
6. Do you know what teaching styles are employed to support learning?	30	30	40
7. Do you know how staff support the development of confident, independent children with positive self-esteem?	60	20	20
8. Do you know how the routines are organised to encourage self-management?	30	40	30
9. Do you know how far staff are sensitive, stimulating and empowering?	40	20	40
10. Do you know how staff engage in negotiations about expectations for learning and behaviour?	20	60	20

What was most striking was the high percentages of 'no ideas' and 'not too sure'.

It was a starting point. Meetings were then held for parents and staff in all the settings to develop partnerships and the best ways to engage boys in learning. Each setting developed a mission statement, with parents, based upon vision and values. They also drew up an action plan to improve knowledge of the issues raised above and how to engage more males in the learning.

Each of the settings invited male visitors and role models to come to the setting. They also introduced ways of encouraging fathers and significant male carers to further develop established relationships with their children: through stay and play, reading activities, shared mark making and practical construction. There was also an emphasis on promoting positive images and resources to reflect male roles and on identifying existing practices and building upon these.

Prior to the questionnaires and meetings, the practitioners in the setting had taken a series of observations of boys, looking at their involvement in learning and the areas of learning that boys were developing and exploring.

Following the briefings and construction of the vision statement the practitioners took a further series of observations to look at the impact of the input and to plan possible ways forward.

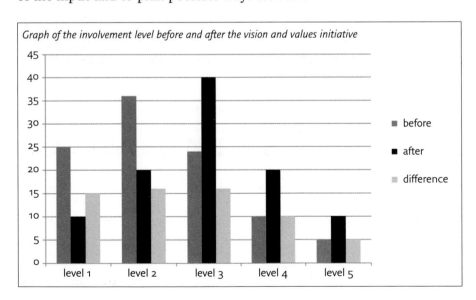

Graph of the involvement level before and after the vision and values initiative

Getting it right for boys

What the graph shows is a huge increase in the percentage of boys who became more involved in learning and doing as a result of good male interaction in the settings – Level 3 involvement rose by 16 per cent, while Level 4 and 5 rose by ten and five per cent respectively.

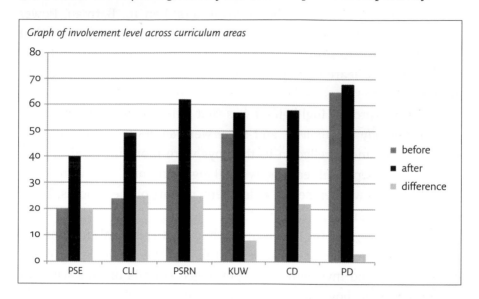

Graph of involvement level across curriculum areas

This graph highlights that the boys, following and during sensitive male engagement, were receiving a more balanced curriculum.

The settings are currently working on action plans to identify which strands of numeracy and literacy the boys were most engaged with and which ones less so, and what elements of personal and social education were strengths and which still require support and development. Initial findings are showing that:

- Disposition and Attitudes has increased
- Language for Thinking has improved
- Shape, Space and Measure is now more integral to the learning day both indoors and outdoors.

The settings are taking the research further by developing the outdoor learning possibilities. It is an ongoing research model and one that I strongly recommend that you employ in your setting or school if you are serious about making an impact on boys' learning.

I am not arguing here that boys will only become truly involved if there are positive male role models in the setting. The point of the project was to highlight how different mindsets either negate learning or allow it to flourish. What practitioners need to do more than anything else is to step aside from the actual play and look at the actual learning that is going on – they may be Transformers, Ben 10, Batman, Power Rangers – and you may not like this play, or deem it inappropriate, but you are not going to stop it. Embrace it, live it, have fun with it and start to diagnose the learning within it and then extend that learning into other fields.

What the project highlighted was that when there was a sense of *'Yes we can play in this way'* and there were adults who supported it, challenged it, and revelled in it, the boys were more involved in their learning. So deep-level learning was taking place, and they were more confident and saw themselves as learners, as part of the process, being done *with* not done *to*.

To work alongside the observation schedule is a physical environment audit tool (see below). As discussed in this and the last chapter, deep-level learning and involvement for prolonged periods of time will only take place if the boys in your setting are emotionally, physically and cognitively secure. So I would recommend that you and your team audit your physical environment, and also audit your routines. Are they conducive to learning for your boys? If not CHANGE THEM!

PHYSICAL ENVIRONMENT

Name of setting _____

The 'inside environment'

1. Dimensions of the rooms used for children in your study (in metres).

   _____

2. Rooms and their purpose.

   _____

   _____

   _____

3. (a) Arrangement of space (inside). Please sketch how you arrange the rooms you use.

(b) State briefly why your room(s) are set out like this.

_____

_____

4. Tick if you have any of the following:

☐ soft furnishings
☐ a place for children's belongings
☐ facilities for changing and washing
☐ child-size toilets
☐ hot and cold running water
☐ sleeping area
☐ physical movement area
☐ community/parents room
☐ office
☐ displays

☐ accessible facilities for independence and self help
☐ quiet area
☐ wheelchair access, space for special chairs
☐ laundry, washing facilities
☐ kitchen
☐ meals, dining facilities
☐ staff (e.g. staff room, separate toilet facilities)
☐ telephone

5. Tick if you have access to the following:

☐ water, play equipment
☐ computers/IT
☐ books
☐ cooking
☐ woodwork
☐ construction (large blocks)
☐ home corner/imaginative play
☐ movement/physical (e.g. climbers, Quadro)
☐ other materials (please state)
☐ writing materials
☐ nature

☐ miniature world
☐ musical instruments
☐ pets
☐ art/creative materials
☐ sensory equipment for visually or hearing impaired children
☐ sand
☐ dressing-up clothes
☐ puzzles, jigsaws
☐ audio equipment
☐ small construction (e.g. Duplo, Sticklebricks)

The 'outside environment'

6. (a) Have you access to an outside area? ☐ Yes ☐ No

    (b) If yes, how often do you use the outside area?

    _____

    _____

7. Is it shared? ☐ Yes ☐ No

    How is it shared?

    _____

    _____

    With whom?

    _____

8. How is the area supervised?

    _____

    _____

9. Sketch how you use the outside area.

10. Please indicate if you have any of the following:

☐ outside games   ☐ wheeled toys

☐ garden/scented garden   ☐ pets/nature study

☐ sand/water pit   ☐ any other items (please state)

☐ adventure playground   _____

☐ outside storage   _____

☐ climbing frame/slide/swings   _____

The overall environment

11. (a) Please indicate the condition of equipment and facilities in percentage form:

    _____ old, work, needs replacing

    _____ well used, but in working order

    _____ new, recent, in excellent condition

    (b) Comments:

    _____

    _____

Getting it right for boys

12. (a) Are the equipment and facilities sufficient for the number of children catered for?

☐ Yes ☐ No

(b) Comments:

_____

_____

13. Describe the provision for security and safety:

(a) For adults:

_____

_____

(b) For children:

_____

_____

(c) For equipment and resources:

_____

_____

In conclusion

Hopefully this book will have given you a brief glimpse into how males work and how and why boys respond as they do. Please enjoy the boys in your schools and settings. Make it your mission to involve as many males in your setting as possible – it adds another dimension and allows boys to be with a role model. How many times have you said of a student or male helper, *'The kids love him'* – well yes they do, they also love you, but he is just that little bit different and might see things in a slightly different and innate way when the mud-eating monsters are planning their next exciting caper!

Boys are not underachieving or failing. It is that circumstances and targets have changed. We need to get some perspective on this issue and let boys be as they are and not compare them to girls in terms of attainment, this just adds stress to everybody. Good practitioners value the difference between genders as much as they do within genders. Sensible differentiation of expectation, support and deep practitioner knowledge will allow boys to achieve their full potential and to see themselves as capable, confident and creative learners.

Enjoy – it is supposed to be fun!

Bibliography and further reading

Biddulph, Steve *Raising Boys*. Australia: Finch (2010) London: Harper Thorsons (2010)

Biddulph, Steve (2010) *The New Manhood.* Australia: Finch

Blum, D (1997) *Sex on the Brain: The biological differences between men and women.* New York: Viking

Boys' and Young Men's Health: Literature and Practice Review (2001) An interim report carried out by Working With Men (Trefor Lloyd and Simon Forrest) on behalf of the Health Development Agency, London

Bredekamp, Sue and Copple, Carol (1997) *Developmentally Appropriate Practice in Early Childhood Programs Serving Children from Birth through Age 8.* National Association for the Education of Young Children

Chief Medical Officers of England, Scotland, Wales, and Northern Ireland (2011) *Start Active, Stay Active: a report on physical activity from the four home countries' Chief Medical Officers,* Department of Health

Cohen-Bendahan, C C C, van de Beek, C, and Berenbaum, S A (2005) 'Prenatal sex hormone effects on child and adult sex- typed behavior: Methods and findings'. *Neuroscience and Biobehavioral Reviews* 29, 353-384.

Corbett, P (2007) *Bumper Book of story Telling into Writing: Key Stage 1.* London: Clown Publishing

Csikszentmihalyi, Mihaly (2000) *Beyond Boredom and Anxiety: Experiencing flow in work and play* (25th Anniversary Edition) San Francisco: Jossey Bass

Csikszentmihalyi, Mihaly and Jackson, Susan A (1999) *Flow in Sports: The keys to optimal experiences and performances.* Champaign, Illinois: Human Kinetics Publisher

Deci, E L (1975) *Intrinsic Motivation.* New York: Plenum Publishing Co

DCSF (2007) *Confident, Capable and Creative: Supporting boys' achievements*

DCSF *Talk for Writing* (2008)

DCSF (2009) *Learning, Playing and Interacting: Good practice in the Early Years Foundation Stage*

DCSF (2009) *Gender and Education: Gapbusters*

DCSF (2009) *Gender and Education – Mythbusters*

DfES (2007) *The Early Years Foundation Stage*

DfES (2001) *Promoting Children's Mental Health within Early Years and School Settings*

Dweck, C S (1999) *Self-theories: Their role in motivation, personality and development.* Philadelphia: Psychology Press

Dweck, C S (2006) *Mindset: The new psychology of success.* New York: Random House

Eden, Anthony (1960) (1962) (1965) *The Memoirs of the Rt. Hon. Sir Anthony Eden KG, PC, MC: Full Circle.* (3 volumes) London: Cassell

Education and Care in the 21st century: International perspectives, pp. 236–251. Cedar Falls, IA: Martin Quam Press

Getting it right for boys

Fausto-Sterling, Anne (1992) *Myths of Gender: biological theories about women and men.* New York: BasicBooks

Goddard-Blythe, Sally (2009) *Attention, Balance and Co-ordination: The A. B. C of learning success.* (First edition) New Jersey: Wiley-Blackwell

Grolnick, W S, and Ryan, R M (1989) 'Parent styles associated with children's self-regulation and competence in schools'. *Journal of Educational Psychology* 81 143-154

Gurian, M, Henley, P, and Trueman, T (2001) *Boys and Girls Learn Differently! A guide for teachers and parents.* San Francisco: Jossey-Bass/John Wiley

Hartley, B and Sutton, R (2010) *Children's Development of Stereotypical Gender-related Expectations about Academic Engagement and Consequences for Performance.* Masters dissertation paper

Havers, F (1995) 'Rhyming tasks male and female brains differently'. *The Yale Herald*, Inc. New Haven, CT: Yale University

Holland, Penny (2003) *We Don't Play with Guns Here: War, weapons and superhero play in the early years*, Maidenhead: Open University Press

I CAN (2006) *The Cost to the Nation of Children's Poor Communication* Response to the Review of Early Years and Childcare Workforce, I Can Talk series Issue 3. London: I CAN

Jordan, E (1995). 'Fighting boys and fantasy play: The construction of masculinity in the early years of school'. *Gender and Education*, 7, 69-86.

Kamii, C, and Kato, Y (2006) 'Early childhood education based on Piaget's constructivism' in Takeuchi, M, and Scott, R (Eds) *New Directions for Early Childhood*

Kamii C (1984) *Autonomy: The Aim of Education Envisioned by Piaget* The Phi Delta Kappan, Vol. 65, No. 6, 410-415

Koestner, R (2008) 'Reaching one's personal goals: A motivational perspective focused on autonomy'. *Canadian Psychology* 49 (1) (2008) 60-67

Laevers, F (1994) 'The innovative project Experiential Education and the definition of quality in education' in: Laevers F (ed.), *Defining and Assessing Quality in Early Childhood Education. Studia Paedagogica*, Leuven University Press, 159-172

Laevers, F (1998) 'Understanding the world of objects and of people: Intuition as the core element of deep level learning'. *International Journal of Educational Research*, 29 (1), 69-85

Laevers, F (2000) 'Forward to basics! Deep-level-learning and the experiential approach'. *Early Years*, 20 (2) 2000.

Laevers, F (2005). 'The curriculum as means to raise the quality of early childhood education: Implications for policy'. *European Early Childhood Education Research Journal*, 13 (1), 17-30.

McCarthy, M M and Arnold, A P (2007) 'Sex differences in the brain: What's old and what's new' in: *Sex Differences in the Brain: From Genes to Behavior*, (Eds) Becker, J B, Berkley, K J, Geary, N, Hampson, E, Herman J and Young E. Oxford: Oxford University Press

Millard, Elaine (1997) *Differently Literate: Boys and girls and the schooling of literacy.* London: Routledge and Farmer

Moir A and Jessel D (1989) *Brain Sex: The real difference between men and women* New York: Bantam Doubleday Dell Publishing Group; 2nd edition

NICE (2007) *Promoting Children's Social and Emotional Wellbeing in Primary Education*

Nucci, Larry, Killen, Melanie and Smetana, Judith (1996) 'Autonomy and the personal: Negotiation and social reciprocity in adult-child social exchanges' *New Directions for Child and Adolescent Development* Volume 1996, Issue 73

O'Neill, Brendan 'Beyond the boy zone' Reproduced from *LM* magazine, issue 120, May 1999

O'Sullivan, Jack (1997) 'Education: A bad way to educate boys' *The Independent* newspaper (3rd April)

Paley, Vivian (1984) *Boys and Girls: Superheroes in the Doll Corner* Chicago: University of Chicago Press

Paley, Vivian (1988) *Bad Guys Don't Have Birthdays: Fantasy play at four* Chicago: University of Chicago Press

Paley, Vivian (2007) *On Listening to What the Children Say* Journal *Harvard Educational Review* Harvard Education Publishing Group Volume 77, Number 2 Summer 2007, 152-163

Parker, L H and Rennie, L J (1995). *For the Sake of Girls?* Final report of the Western Australian single-sex education pilot project 1993-1994. Report prepared for the Education Department of Western Australia, Perth. National Key Centre for Teaching and Research in School Science and Mathematics, Perth: Curtin University of Technology

Piaget, Jean and Elkind, David (Ed) (1970) *Six Psychological Studies.* New York: John Wiley

Pirsig, Robert, (1984) *Zen and the Art of Motor Cycle Maintenance* New York: Bantam

QCA (2008) *Early Years Foundation Stage Profile Handbook*

Rich, B. (Ed) (2000) *The Dana Brain Daybook.* New York: The Charles A Dana Foundation

Rogers, Carl (1961) *On Becoming a Person: A therapist's view of psychotherapy.* London: Constable

Rogers, Carl (1969) *Freedom to Learn: A View of What Education Might Become.* (First edition) Columbus, Ohio: Charles Merill

Rogers, Carl (1980) *A Way of Being.* Boston: Houghton Mifflin

Ruble, D N, Martin, C L and Berenbaum, S A (2006). 'Gender development'. In Damon W (Series Ed) and Eisenberg N (Vol. Ed), *Handbook of Child Psychology* (6th edition, Vol. 3, 858-932). New York: Wiley

Siraj-Blatchford et al, (2002) *Researching Effective Pedagogy in the Early Years* (REPEY) Institute of Education, University of London; Department of Educational Studies, University of Oxford; DfES

Strachota, Bob (1996) *On Their Side: Helping children take charge of their learning.* Greenfield MA: Northeast Foundation for Children

Taylor, John R (2002) *Cognitive Grammar.* Oxford Textbooks in Linguistics, Oxford: Oxford University Press

The New Zealand Curriculum (2007) Ministry of Education;, Wellington, New Zealand: Learning Media Limited

Venger, Leonid (1967), cited in Veraksa, Nikolay E. *International Journal of Early Years Education,* Volume 19, Number 1, 1 March 2011 , 79-87(9). London: Routledge

Vygotsky, L S (1967) Play and its role in the mental development of the child. *Soviet Psychology,* 5 (3) 6-18. (Original work published 1966)

Vygotsky, L (1987) *The Collected Works of LS Vygotsky* New York: Plenum Press

Walkerdine, V (1983) 'It's only natural: rethinking child-centred pedagogy' in Wolpe, A M and Donald J (eds) *Is There Anyone Here from Education?* London: Pluto Press

Wilson, Gary (2007) *Raising Boys' Achievement* (illustrated edition) London: Network Continuum Education